AMSTERDAM IN DETAIL

Amsterdam in detail

Edited by Maarten Kloos

ARCAM/Architectura & Natura Press

Editor
Maarten Kloos
Text editors
Birgitte de Maar, H.J. Scheepmaker
Production
Maarten Kloos, Birgitte de Maar
Translated by
Jane Zuyl-Moores
Design
Typography & Other Serious Matters
Printing
Drukkerij Rob Stolk, Amsterdam
Publisher
ARCAM, in conjunction with
Architectura & Natura Press, Amsterdam

ISBN 90 71570 74 6

*Published with the financial support of
Stimuleringsfonds voor Architectuur, Rotterdam,
and the City of Amsterdam
(Department of Art and Culture)*

CONTENTS

CONTENTS

INTRODUCTION

The detail and the cityscape: it is a natural and yet, remarkably enough, little-investigated combination. Although there is extensive literature on most (architectural and other) details, it seldom does full justice to the richness of the detail, because almost invariably only one aspect of the detail is discussed; for example, typology, constructional principles or decorative quality. This prompted ARCAM to look at the urban detail in all its complexity, or rather, to examine and analyse the urban experience at the level of the detail.

It became apparent to us at a very early stage in the preparation of this book that the subject is far more complex than we had supposed. Initially, we had a clear idea of what the book would be about, the subject seemed easy to define. It was to be about details visible from the public space. Discussions with friends and relations yielded the following examples: the (sharp) street corner, the leaning façade, the entrance with porch, the neglected first floor, brick patterns, the wall

*Housing,
Minervalaan*
[J. Rooden-
burgh, 1932]

anchor, the sash window, the nineteenth-century stone accent, the hoisting beam, the roof landscape, the annexation of part of the street by residents, the grey paving stone, the design of the relationship with the water (the jetty, the pontoon, the floating garden).

In subsequent discussions we tried to name sub-themes and find a system, with the remarkable result that the questions increased in number.

Imagery · The urban detail is part of the imagery of the city at the level of composition and subtle phrasing. It also has to do with abstract concepts such as scale, sight lines and the routes city dwellers follow (for example, Amsterdam changes in a severe winter when the canals freeze over and you can walk across them). It is also about acoustics, because the city sounds different in different places and in different weather conditions (the sound in sunny weather is quite different from the sound in rain or snow), the sound traffic makes on clinkers is different from the sound it makes on asphalt. Detail is moreover a very personal subject. While in Amsterdam-Zuid (H.P. Berlage, 1917) most people's attention is usually drawn to the façades or the beautiful relief of the window frames (see the housing blocks on Minervalaan by J. Roodenburgh, 1932), the Dutch singer Mathilde Santing, when describing this her favourite neighbourhood, once expressed her surprise at the way in which 'the colour of the leaves matches that of the stones'.

Further, it is important that objects are able to generate a new use. A good example is the masterly way in which Amsterdammers (particularly proprietors of outdoor cafés) deal with the simple posts (the so-called 'Amsterdammertjes') designed to prevent motorists from parking on the pavement. The urban detail also of course evokes memories; memories of certain atmospheres experienced – youth with its secret places, the war, the period of the postwar reconstruction, the sixties, popular celebrations such as 'koninginnedag' (the queen's birthday) or when the Ajax football team wins a championship.

As soon as a certain detail becomes connected with a lifestyle, there is the problem of interpretation. For example, the fact that the Dutch do not draw their curtains in the evening amazes every first-time visitor to the country, but is something the Dutch themselves are barely conscious of. In the evening, the interiors of Dutch dwellings become a visual part of the public urban space. However, no one knows whether this is because the Dutch simply have nothing to hide, or are so frugal that they like to read in the evening by the light of the street lamps.

The way in which people look at the city is linked to what strikes the eye and is remembered. From which elements in the city do we derive our image of the city?

The touristic image · In general, this image is the familiar touristic image. For many people, Amsterdam is synonymous with the Dam, the large monuments, the canals, the Amstel and the IJ. However, this makes the search for other, less obvious images all the more interesting.

If we look at the way in which Amsterdam figures in literature, what strikes us most is that, here too, clichés play a role. Writing from abroad at the beginning of this century, the Dutch writer Neel Doff expressed her longing for Amsterdam. She missed ' [...] Herengracht and its dark, stately houses with their double steps, enclosed with chains and wrought ironwork, [...] the high-backed stone bridges where beneath the arches you saw the reflection of the houses with their sculpted doors and steps' (Annelies de Korver, ed., *Het Amsterdam van ...* , Amsterdam, 1995).

In other texts, the city functions as a backdrop. For example, in one of Remco Campert's novels, the main character arrives in Amsterdam in the square in front of Centraal Station. Campert gives a perfect description of the square – which is in fact not a square but a transport interchange – just by mentioning the pedestrian route, a zebra crossing and a traffic light. The situation is the same with regard to films. Some films present a clichéd image of the city (see the French film *Barocco* by André Téchiné, of 1976, with Isabelle Adjani as a prostitute). Others capture the essence of Amsterdam. In *Alice in den Städten* (Wim Wenders, 1974), the main characters stay one night in Amsterdam and know where to find a good restaurant: a legendary Chinese restaurant (which no longer exists and was known only to insiders because it was hidden behind the kitchen in the basement) in the centre of the old city.

Questions · An examination of the detail raises questions thus. Questions about detail as a typological phenomenon. What is the essence of the detail? In what theoretical context should we see Amsterdam's cityscape, taking into consideration the detailing of its architecture and urban space? Questions about detail as the embodiment of architectural messages and as a source of information, enabling us to identify architectural styles, ideologies and the chronology of architectural history. Questions about the background to the historical image of a city like Amsterdam with its many monuments. How do all these historical details fit together constructionally?

What does detail mean to the architect? Is it of the essence (an essential aspect of the materialization of the design) or merely the final result, at the end of the line? How important is detail in the management and restoration of our historical heritage, and what does detail say about the current state of affairs as regards the structures of buildings? What is the quality of 'constructionally sophisticated' details, and how do designers and builders deploy them?

There are also of course questions relating to the urban space. What role does detail play in the experience of this space? How important are aspects such as choice of material, texture, differences in the level of the pavement, and the layer of details consisting of all

kinds of messages (commercial messages, for example), as a result of which the city is a medium? What is the significance of detail for the experience of the city and the city image in all its complexity, and for the collective memory? Why are some details an emotional link and thus important as a reference, while others are never more than a neutral element present in the city? Is there in this respect a difference between the experiences of the professional and the lay person, and between the response of the Amsterdammer and that of the tourist?

Attention · It is a noteworthy fact that, in addition to general images, people easily remember pregnant details – often more easily than the buildings of which the details are part. Remarkably enough, there is a revival of interest in the detail, particularly among young designers. After Mies van der Rohe's pathetic 'God is in the detail', the generation of Rem Koolhaas and Bernard Tschumi introduced architecture without details. For the most part, the younger generation of architects eschews such flirtations and, together with a renewed interest in construction, shows a down-to-earth and practical interest in good detailing. Consequently, the subject has a certain topicality.

Getting the experts to talk about detail was not easy. Steven Holl, for example, who is a regular visitor to Amsterdam because he is to build a large housing block in the city, did not have time for even a brief statement. In the period in which he was working on his design for the housing block on KNSM island, Hans Kollhoff became fascinated by certain details, such as the sash window (see Maurits Klaren, ed., *Piraeus – een woongebouw van Kollhoff*, Rotterdam, 1994). He declined to go more deeply into it for this ARCAM POCKET. During one of his frequent visits to the Berlage Institute in Amsterdam, we asked Kenneth Frampton to contribute some observations on the detail. He later, on the telephone from New York, said he would like to write about 'those villas next to Herman Hertzberger's schools on Apollolaan, in Amsterdam-Zuid'. He was obviously visualizing them with their bricks and tiles, and their sculptural oriels. He also wondered why he remembered those houses in particular. However, we did not receive a text from him.

The inescapable detail · Why do these people have such difficulty in putting their thoughts down on paper? Some of them (Frampton, for instance) were willing to express themselves on the subject over the telephone. Perhaps fear plays a part, because while distance in this world of virtual realities has become a relative concept, study of the detail leads directly to the realization that the tangible detail is unavoidable. Like gravity: you can play with it, but you cannot completely avoid it.

In order to provide insight into the complexity, we asked diverse authors to contribute a text. Dutch designers such as Ben van Berkel & Caroline Bos, Kees Christiaanse, Felix Claus & Kees Kaan, Jo Coenen, Aldo van Eyck, Adriaan Geuze, Herman Hertzberger, Sjoerd Soeters, Joop van Stigt, Dirk Sijmons and René van Zuuk. Foreign designers who are realizing projects in and around Amsterdam (Sven-Ingvar Andersson, Joan Busquets, Roger Diener, Peter Ellis, Gordon Haslett, Antonio Ortiz and Renzo Piano). In addition, an architect turned publicist/theorist (Stan Allen),

*Villa,
Apollolaan*
[Gulden &
Geldmaker,
1928]

a structural engineer (Harry Evers), a politician responsible for public space (Guusje ter Horst), two historians (Aart Oxenaar and Henk Zantkuijl) and four outsiders (sculptor Norman Dilworth, journalist Henk Hofland, Neerlandist Bernt Luger, and John Thackara, director of the Netherlands Design Institute).

Together, these authors have produced a book which is more impressionistic than we had expected; a book which does not so much explain as stimulate the reader to look with close attention at the city. Some people are of the opinion that the city of the future – to quote from William Gibson's book *Neuromancer* (1984) – will resemble night-time Los Angeles, seen from a height of 1,500 metres. This book, however, maintains the reverse: look at the city with your nose pressed against the window.

MAARTEN KLOOS

Rivierenbuurt · The house where I was born stood in the neighbourhood 'Rivierenbuurt', and as a child I used to think that all cities were like it. You don't know any better. It is a monumental neighbourhood with a clear hierarchy. There are three wide avenues and side streets which themselves have side streets. The neighbourhood becomes more intimate and pleasant, is increasingly given over to dwelling, with every corner you turn. The streets have the right width, so that, where necessary, you have contact with the opposite side, which produces a room-like effect.

I used to think the block opposite our house was very ugly. It was only much later that I discovered that this was because of the rows of badly designed windows, the continuous gutter and the ungainly roof above it. I still dream about that block, but probably for a different reason. Here in 1940, I saw the Germans enter the city, and some of my friends were deported in the war. It is impossible to dissociate yourself from buildings and people and your memories of them. I also remember that in Vrijheidslaan, near the building the 'Wolkenkrabber' (Skyscraper), of 1930, by J.F. Staal, the tram used to run on the wrong side through the grass: antiauthoritarian and impressive.

The neighbourhood has splendid, monumental porches with stone staircases and at the top, four, five or six doors. Everyone here has their own front door, and there are the most fantastic variants. I remember the stone eggs at the foot of the steps. If my memory is correct they used to be much smoother, and I could never resist the temptation to go and sit on them. They were not very comfortable, but they gave you a sense of the physicalness of architecture, that architecture can become part of yourself.

An unusual feature is that some of the houses here have a walled front garden, a sort of balcony on the ground floor. It is quite possible that as an architect I was strongly influenced by the garden wall, behind which I grew up and felt secure. Perhaps the oriels with their slanting windows played a part too. No one in the Rivierenbuurt looks out on a blind wall, every window affords a reasonable view. Architecturally, this is perhaps unimportant, but there are so very many such, in themselves, unimportant elements that together they have resulted in something important.

AMSTERDAM IN DETAIL
HENK HOFLAND

Projecting below the ridge of many Amsterdam roofs is a thick, horizontal beam; an addition which has nothing to do with the aesthetic theories of the Golden Age, neoclassicism or functionalism. It is a detail in the totality of the urban landscape. The visitor to Amsterdam notices these beams everywhere, along the canals and in the working-class districts – long rows of gibbet-like projections which the uninitiated may surmise have been placed there in anticipation of the next revolution. *A la lanterne!*

For Amsterdammers born and bred, these are everyday objects: hoisting beams, hooked projections for use when moving house. However, they can serve other purposes, examples of which are to be found in Dutch literature. I quote the writer R.J. Peskens from his short story 'Ik zou graag eens met u willen spreken' (in: *Vlissingse verhalen*, Amsterdam, 1995) in which a hoisting beam fulfils a surprising function: 'When Ben finally mentioned his name, I immediately remembered his father hanging, a rope around his neck, from the short hoisting beam at the top of the front wall. He just stepped out of the pivoting window, people said when they asked each other how it had happened.'

Anyone who has not grown up with the hoisting beam and has never asked what it is for, discovers its function when in front of the house with the beam they see a piano, table or bed hanging from a rope. Anything else hanging from the rope is an exception.

Moving house · A number of things can be inferred from the presence of so many hoisting beams. For a start, it says something about Amsterdam staircases: they are narrower than narrow. The projecting section of most beams is no longer than about 75 centimetres. From this we can conclude that Amsterdam removal men have a special hoisting technique: they often use two ropes. The first rope is attached to the object, the second rope is used in order to prevent the object from grazing a wall or window.

The hoisting beam is a good example of an informal, functional architectural element which has become a characteristic detail, rather like the small water tower on American roofs which tells us all sorts of things about the American water supply. The hoisting beam, too, comes in all shapes and sizes: the ornamented beam of the Golden Age, the late-nineteenth-century beam with its splendid ornamental ironwork (a fine example can be seen on the corner of Lijnbaansgracht and Vijzelgracht), the simple steel beam in the nineteenth- and twentieth-century working-class districts.

Hoisting

People with an above-average eye for detail are inclined to regard phenomena such as hoisting beams and water towers as main items. They then become prey to overconcentration and finally a collector of some sort. There are, for example, tourists who go to Amsterdam chiefly in order to photograph hoisting beams with their telephoto lenses.

Bollards · Amsterdam probably has more bollards than any other city in the world. They are designed to prevent motorists from parking where this is not allowed. Over the years, the Amsterdam bollard has undergone a development.

The first model has a rounded top bearing an embellishment and the city's coat of arms. This beautiful piece of street furniture is called an Amsterdammertje. This model was followed by a simpler version – a thin, cylindrical bollard with a plain ring as an ornament around the flattened top. However, even a few hundred thousand of these Amsterdammertjes, it seems, were unable to tame the motorist. For this reason, stone bollards, which come in three types, were introduced. In addition, elongated blocks, measuring about twenty centimetres by one metre, were placed along the edge of footways and were painted yellow to prevent pedestrians from tripping over them.

Other cities have their own ways of stopping motorists from parking where this is not allowed. In Paris, kerbs are so high that no motorist would risk damaging his or her sump on them. In New York, which enforces its regulation on the towing away of illegally parked cars more rigorously than any other city in the world (with the exception of Singapore perhaps), signs read

Amsterdam-mertjes

'Don't even think of parking here'. Amsterdam – with little regard for aesthetic considerations presumably – has opted for a method which is most reminiscent of passive military defences: permanent iron and concrete barriers.

This has had inevitable consequences for the city-scape: highly characteristic of Amsterdam is the over-turned bollard. The original Amsterdammertjes lend the city a rustic air. Take, for example, the 'old' Leidse-plein, the public space between the Stadsschouwburg (city theatre) and the entrance to Leidsestraat. The street frontage – particularly on the side with the small houses that look as if they are made of gingerbread – is in itself highly rustic in appearance. And this rustic feel is decisively reinforced by the presence in the square of some five hundred Amsterdammertjes.

If Walt Disney had sent Mickey Mouse to Amster-dam, then the old Leidseplein would undoubtedly have been the scene of his adventures. The Dutch have their

*Rear
balconies*

*Front
balcony*
➤

own Walt Disney, not a world-famous figure, but a household name in the Netherlands: the artist Anton Pieck. With its Amsterdammertjes, the old Leidseplein might have been designed by him.

Balconies · Amsterdam is also a city of balconies – rear balconies and front balconies. The rear balconies have no aesthetic function whatsoever: they are rectangular spaces onto which two doors open: the back-room (or the bedroom) door and the kitchen door. This balcony usually has a rail with posts, which creates a barred effect. The rail is used for hanging sheets, blankets and rugs over – the sheets and blankets in order to 'air' them, and the rugs in order to beat them. Consequently, the balcony is an inbuilt cause of vertical neighbours' quarrels: the occupants of the ground-floor flat are showered with the dust beaten out of the rugs of their upstairs neighbours. In addition, the balcony usually has a built-in wooden cupboard, in which

Windows as parallelo- grams

the Dutch keep objects they mistakenly believe may one day come in handy. This cupboard is usually situated next to the kitchen door, near which stands the dustbin. Last but not least, the balcony is where the cat box is kept.

A characteristic feature of housing in Amsterdam is that most houses are built in rows around an open space which is subdivided into gardens where semi-wild flora and fauna flourish. Because – as I have already mentioned – the balcony railings have a barred appearance, anyone who has the opportunity to view rows of balconies (three or four above each other) will, depending on the time of year, imagine one of two things: in the winter, that he or she is in an open prison, and in the summer that he or she is standing on the edge of a sort of urban woods.

Balconies on the front of Amsterdam houses are rare. Those that exist are smaller than rear balconies and are not immediately noticeable. They are seldom if ever used, which not only has to do with the climate, but also with the Dutch national character. Generally, the full-blown balcony on the façade belongs to a great rhetorical tradition. The Amsterdam front balcony, in contrast to the Roman, French or Belgian balcony, is, all things considered, a rudiment. There are no great demagogues in the Netherlands, not even in Amsterdam, and this has always been the case. The Dutch do not deliver orations, they hold meetings, and the latter is not possible on a balcony.

Decay · A curious phenomenon (which, as it were, happens to the architecture in Amsterdam) is the lopsided house. It is a product of weak ground, low-rise and the conservation of buildings.

Piles have to be sunk for every building in Amsterdam and in some cases, with the passage of time – sometimes decades, sometimes centuries – the foundations slowly begin to give way. The process of decay is so gradual that the masonry does not always fracture, but often appears to be able to adapt to the situation. In some cases, the building has subsided to such an extent that it seems to defy the laws of gravity. Had it been high-rise, the structure would long since have collapsed. Low-rise, up to two or three storeys, appears to be capable of withstanding the pressure. Windows become improbable parallelograms.

Then, in the nick of time, the government's concern for the national heritage is aroused and therefore the building is shored up. The shores usually remain in place for several years, during which time they become weathered, moss establishes itself on the wood, ironwork rusts, and grass and weeds start to grow in cracks

and crannies. Thus, the shores for the historic monument themselves become a monument to the proposed conservation.

Methods · With regard to all of the above, the detail – which was produced neither for architectural nor for aesthetic reasons – has to be discovered. There are special methods for going about this. In Amsterdam, do not concentrate on prospects of canals, rows of façades and the totality of the cityscape. Rather, either look upwards as much as possible or keep your eyes close to the ground.

In the first case, there is a special surprise in store. Look skywards in the narrow streets of Amsterdam's city centre and you will see the contrasts between the ages. The city lives. This means that retailers hold their own and express their vitality by constantly revamping the ground floor of their shops. In key shopping streets such as Leidsestraat, Kalverstraat and Utrechtsestraat, above the wide plate-glass windows of contemporary shop fronts rises the masonry of past centuries, crowned with stepped and Dutch gables.

Anyone with an eye for architecture will discover here the dividing line between the various periods: the few remnants of late-nineteenth-century cast- and wrought-ironwork, Art Nouveau, functionalism, commercial postmodernism. And all of this beneath the roofs by the great master builders of the seventeenth century who, after all, have determined the character and appearance of Amsterdam's centre to this day.

Contrasting ages

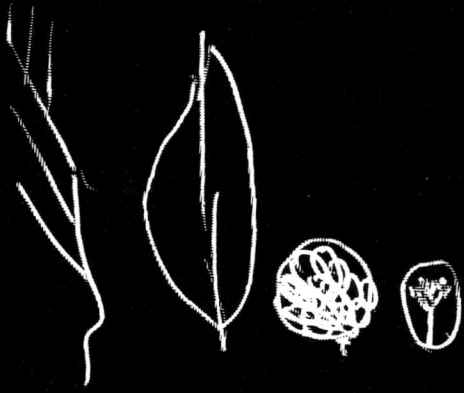

Presently · Of course, everyone thinks that the character of Amsterdam is determined by its canals and the districts around the city centre. However, although the bridges, the beautiful façades and the Royal Palace create a special ambience, they do not constitute the essence of the city. Like every real city, Amsterdam is determined by the mentality of its inhabitants. With their characteristic boisterousness and excessive self-assurance, the Amsterdammers are the essence of Amsterdam.

This is Amsterdam.

Most of the time, this excessive self-assurance manifests itself in smart-alec behaviour and griping. When the weather is bad, this gives rise to a morose and aggressive atmosphere in the streets. Everyone gets in each other's way and expresses their irritation in surly looks and gestures. In the summer, the atmosphere is different. The city is vibrant and a bravado takes hold of the Amsterdammers. This mood, which is experienced as convivial, can become sultry with everyone flirting with everyone else.

The question urges itself upon us as to what is directing these two extreme manifestations of the Amsterdam soul and is the decisive factor in bringing about this change in the collective mood? Whoever has the key to this change could govern the city.

The answer is simple and disarming.

Early in March, when the city is still grey and windy, the crocuses suddenly burst from the mud. They are few in number but, at once absolutely manifest and fragile, they take possession of Museumplein, the Wetering roundabout and the fields around the Tropeninstituut. Although climatically incorrect, they proclaim a new season. Amsterdammers are confused but the effect is clear. In the city, the cafés put out tables and chairs, the women put on skirts and frocks, the entire city is exuberant. The multicoloured flowers with their white centres are the signal for summer to start. In March!

Of course, there are always people who view the new season with misgivings and continue to grumble. But then presently the elm trees sprout seeds, and millions of seeds hang like socks in their branches. In early April, the seed falls to the ground. The streets and pavements are green, the drains are blocked, the Amsterdammers drunk.

SEEN FROM THE CITY
JOOP VAN STIGT

It is a well-known fact that architectural and constructional detail is often judged by its decorative aspects, whereby it is conveniently forgotten that the detail is usually determined by functional considerations, the available building material and possible methods of construction. However, the same can be said with regard to Amsterdam's urban structure. Few people realize, for example, that the canals – nowadays admired chiefly for their beauty – first and foremost constitute the functional system on the basis of which Amsterdam was able, within a short space of time, to develop from a fishing village into an important mercantile city.

It is therefore good to focus attention on the significance of the phenomenon of detail in the city, and I shall do that here with the words of Charles Eames in mind: 'The detail determines the quality.' An additional motivation is that within the space of a few decades the building industry has changed unbelievably as regards scale and production processes.

Growth of Amsterdam [circum-ference is *circa* 6 x R]

The building task · The main element of the current building task consists of transforming our cities, villages and buildings and thus of renewing their components. This is not new, for the earliest history of architecture provides fascinating examples of new purposes for, and the recycling of, elements of buildings. Many cities acquired a special significance due to forms of transformation. Take, for example, the city of Split, the amphitheatre in Arles, or Granada where, in a quite remarkable way, Roman and Islamic buildings, mosques and stadiums were given a new purpose. Various famous buildings of the past are composed of elements of older buildings. Thus, the temple behind the colossi of Memnon in Egypt was dismantled in order to be used as a quarry for the temple in Karnak, and columns of older Roman buildings were used in the cistern in Istanbul and in the mosque in Cordoba.

In Amsterdam, the issue of new purposes for and the recycling of buildings is highly topical because many

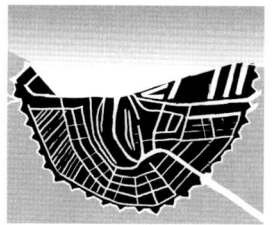 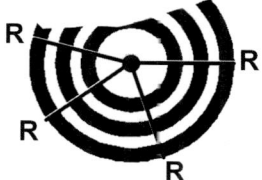

old buildings, which had been built for trade, industry or as hospitals, are in need of qualitative upgrading. This has to be seen in the light of the fact that, unlike many other cities, Amsterdam does not have its origins in castles and palaces built by feudal lords. By about 1600, within the space of fifty years, Amsterdam (which dates from the thirteenth century) had become the world's fourth-largest metropolis. In that period, and afterwards, the city continued to change and has gradually become a unique collage of interesting manifestations of successive cultures and stylistic periods. As a result, Amsterdam reflects both historical developments in art and architecture and social changes of the past. An important characteristic of the city in this respect is the high-quality mix of living, working and recreation, which over the years has become closely linked to a social-democratic tradition.

The transformations that have taken place over some five to six hundred years have brought about and at the same time constantly tested the functional urban concept. And also thanks to a tradition of careful urban planning, the result is a high urban quality. Thus the city still serves as a model for a harmonious entity with a multiplicity of meanings. It is a vibrant and bustling city, important as an economic metropolis. It is also a major tourist centre without being a museum.

Architecture has always complemented the urban concept and has also been notably subservient to the urban public space, the communal space of the city's inhabitants. This holds true for the area within the 'singelgrachten' – the canals encircling the city. (This area is regarded as the historic centre and, with only 15 per cent of the city's buildings, boasts 7,000 listed monuments.) It also holds true for the period after the termination of the 'vestingwet' in 1874, when the city ramparts were demolished and space was created for buildings for trade and industry, which had expanded to such an extent that they could no longer be accommodated within the city centre.

The Dutch house · A distinctive feature of the medieval city was the use of wood. This material was not readily available, but the only material at hand to be used in the marshy ground. Wood determined the load-bearing structure, the parcellation of the canal-side façades and the appearance of the Dutch house. See, for example, 'Het Houten Huys' (wooden house) at 34 Begijnhof, which dates from 1460.

In this period, the wooden frame was usually made in the workshop during the winter months, after which the various components were transported to the building site. Wooden portals were placed one behind the other and stacked in the case of buildings with more than one storey. They consisted of two prefabricated braces which supported tie-beams. Bridging joists were placed in between to support the floorboards or tiles. Roof trusses were stacked on cross-beams and the entire frame was clad with boards.

One of the advantages of the wooden construction with posts, braces and masonry infill was that it required little material. There were, however, drawbacks. Construction was extremely labour-intensive, and in the early days the only wood available was native oak of limited length. It was later when trade with Northern Europe increased and longer and heavier and pinewood could be imported that native oak was supplanted. Construction became simpler because straight beams could now be placed directly on the stone structural wall. Besides, fire prevention more and more called for masonry infill of the wooden framework. The resulting fire walls gradually became supporting walls, which led to an increase of stonework.

The large windows so characteristic of Amsterdam have a distinctive shape which is directly derived from the wooden framework. In fact, all openings are directly related to the frame because they could be created in the wooden façade sections as required. Moreover, the dimensions of the available material and the method of construction gave rise to a natural unity – a unity from which there gradually developed a great diversity, as manifested in the Renaissance architecture of Hendrik de Keyser (1565-1621) and the classicism of architects such as Jacob van Campen (1595-1657) and Philips Vingboons (1607-78). The Dutch house thus developed as a component part of the city.

Het Houten Huys, Begijnhof

The house and the water · Amsterdam's architecture is unquestionably partly determined by the logistic structure of the city. In the cities of antiquity, intersections in the road grid determined the capacity of the transportation of goods ('horse and vehicular' transport). Similarly, Amsterdam's development was for centuries dominated by the system whereby light cargo was conveyed through streets and alleyways to the quays, from where heavy cargo was transported by canal.

The urban expansion of the medieval city was thus still determined by watercourses found in the country. The construction of the ring-shaped expansions of the girdle of canals (Herengracht, Keizersgracht and Prinsengracht) signalled a break; for with this intervention a new pattern was introduced and water, the threatening element, was for the first time converted into a means for development that contributed to Amsterdam's prosperity. The quays were equipped for the transhipment of goods and were linked to the urban system of traffic and transport. This ensured the speedy transhipment of goods and thus an efficient provisioning of the city. Water, carrier of heavy cargo, was directly linked to the dwelling, the top storey and attic of which were used for the storage of goods.

In the development of the old city centre, only public buildings had the privilege to occupy a prominent place in the city. Churches were allowed large volumes and could be orientated towards Jerusalem. Van Campen positioned his town hall (now the Royal Palace) so that it conformed to the waterway of Nieuwezijds Voorburgwal, thereby confirming the urban structure. In the construction of the neighbouring church Nieuwe Kerk,

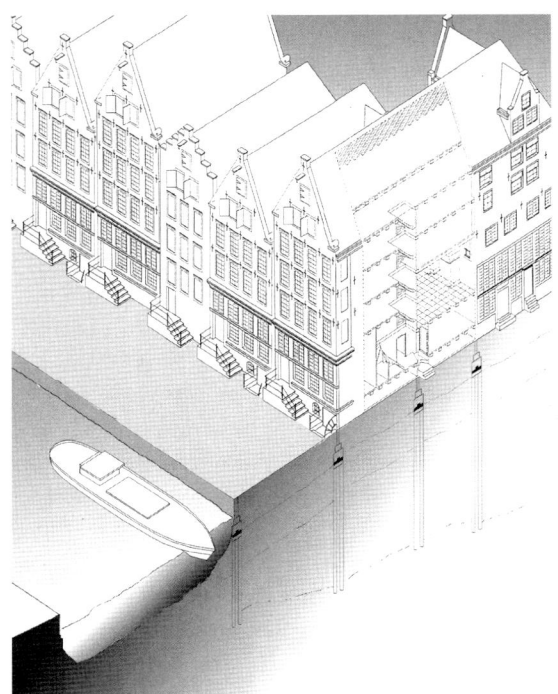

*Profile of
a canal*

the guiding principle was not the urban structure, but the orientation of the building to the east. That the above is not always discernible today is due to the fact that from the end of the nineteenth century onwards, radical alterations were made to the urban structure. Large radial thoroughfares were constructed, canals were filled in and a number of, by Amsterdam standards, extremely large buildings were realized. With their large volumes these buildings soon became landmarks in the city. The Paleis voor Volksvlijt (C. Outshoorn, 1864, destroyed by fire in 1929) and the Rijksmuseum (P.J.H. Cuypers, 1885) became focal points in the city. Furthermore, with their construction, the limits of what the urban fabric was capable of sustaining were fixed.

This was a challenge for urbanists, a challenge designers such as J.G. van Niftrik and H.P. Berlage were eager to take up. Van Niftrik's expansion scheme of 1866 is an attempt to create a new, clear-cut framework. In Berlage's plan for Amsterdam-Zuid, the urbanistic principles and the architectural infill are geared to each other in such a way that they constitute a strong unity; a unity which is also to be found in the treatment of architectural details by the Amsterdam School, whose members (M. de Klerk, J.C. van Epen, D. Greiner and others) were masters at interweaving various functions in a single urban plan – in other words, at making communal facilities such as public buildings and schools subservient to the larger whole.

Changing images · The architectural heritage that came into being in this way creates obligations. Every new generation is confronted with the necessity of maintaining the buildings of previous generations and of renewing components (such as window frames, windows and doors). This holds true for anonymous buildings, but also for monumental canalside houses and treasures such as the Begijnhof (which originally dates from 1346) and housing on P.L. Takstraat and environs by P.L. Kramer and M. de Klerk (1922-23).

In the past, the need to prevent decay has often been used to show changed ideas about living and working. Fashionable ideas, but also changes in status and the fact that increased prosperity brought greater resources played a role. As a result, historic monuments – which are situated in a different context since motor cars and trams replaced the carriages and cargo boats – have seldom retained their original appearance. Successive generations of users have added contemporary elements. Fluted gables were transformed into stepped, neck, Dutch and cornice gables. Storeys were added when extra space was needed. Crossbar window frames were replaced by windows with rods or, later, by the grand Empire window which represented the 'enlightenment'.

Maintenance over the centuries has thus determined the appearance of the cityscape to a considerable extent. The result is a varied and fascinating environment characterized by unity and diversity – at least, there where maintenance has been properly carried out and alterations have been made which attest to the craftsman's natural respect for the products of his predecessors. Where there is an unequivocal use of technical possibilities, the built environment is a true reflection of social relations, ideas about style, and technical possibilities.

In our time too, maintenance, renovation and the recycling of buildings are high on the agenda, if only because of the need to prevent decay. Moreover, we have to guard against being overly eager to demolish buildings which have lost their original function and are therefore redundant. The demolition of buildings which are in a good condition technically can be culturally unjustifiable and undesirable – certainly now that it is recognized that even radical contemporary alterations can be a cultural contribution, provided that they do not show contempt for the existing architecture and harmony takes precedence over contrast. Because no building has ever been developed as a monument, and because a monument has a right to exist only if it is integrated into social use, thinking about new purposes for buildings is an obligation.

In Amsterdam, the new functions of Entrepotdok, Oranje Nassaukazerne and the grain warehouses Korthals Altes show that large-scale projects on the periphery of the old city can become elements which revitalize the surrounding neighbourhoods and link them to the city centre. With their new functions as social and cultural centres, churches such as the Nieuwe Kerk, Posthoornkerk, Vondelkerk, Majella Kerk once again play a role in the city. In all cases, indispensable links have come into being in the chain which is our cultural heritage.

One could say that the urbanistic framework provides unique opportunities for exploiting the remarkable craftsmanship to which our heritage attests, by means of modern techniques. The challenge must be to establish or preserve harmonious connections between contemporary architecture and built history.

Busy elves · Amsterdam is like a city criss-crossed each night by busy elves who stake out and subdivide, trace paths and lay kerbstones. Not an inch of ground escapes their notice.

Such zeal produces surprising results: the general, the public, the standard cede their place to the particular, the private and the singular.

In no other city are there such echoes between house and street. In fact, the space connecting house and canal seems to be laid out as meticulously as the table set for dinner, glimpsed through an adjacent window.

AN AMSTERDAM DELICACY

DIRK SIJMONS

W hoever, by way of pastime, enjoys identifying metropolises (at last a hobby for Rem Koolhaas!) can practise by studying photographs of skylines and famous buildings, or maps of main structures and locations. But for these eccentric metropolis-spotters, the surest clue to the identity of a city are the urban details of the exterior space: telephone boxes, traffic lights, post-boxes, lamp-posts and, last but not least, switch boxes and transformer kiosks.

Although nowadays some of these objects are ordered from catalogues, and there is a certain degree of internationalization, every city has its own combination, often with specially made elements which are immediately recognizable to the practised spotter. I shall resist the temptation to present a chronological and typological classification of the stunning products of Amsterdam's public design of urban details and street furniture.

But whoever should hit upon the idea of producing an identification handbook (for Woodsmen in Highly

Urbanized Areas) would in the chart's main key undoubtedly, as first bifurcation, ask the question:

a. your urban detail has a clear three-dimensionality and stands, hangs or lies in or on the urban space;

b. your urban detail is seemingly two-dimensional and lies horizontally on the surface level or projects slightly above it.

We shall leave 'a' for another occasion and focus in this essay on 'b', the 'Class of covers of drains, of manholes, of mains shafts and of sewers'. If there is an *architecture parlante*, then there will be a soft whispering, and yet these modest urban details have great power of expression. They are the visible manifestation of virtually everything that has to do with the metabolism of the city: intermediaries between the upper world and the lower world.

The simple but beautifully designed cast-iron covers are ornamented with symbols, numbers and cryptic inscriptions such as 'Vecht links' and 'Duin rechts'. As a child, for some time I believed that these were medals awarded to road sweepers in recognition of their work. Most of the medals in the city had evidently been awarded to a certain w (maybe the Trespassers w from *Winnie-the-Pooh*?).

Within the category of covers, let us focus on the family of water mains covers. My personal favourite is also the smallest of its kind: the cast-iron cover measuring 12 by 12 centimetres which is embellished with a capital 'W' and marks the position of a mains-tap in the city's water mains system. A beautiful, flat cover which in busy streets has often been polished by the shoes of passing pedestrians.

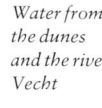

Water from the dunes and the river Vecht

Water supply at the urban level is taken for granted nowadays, but in the past, good-quality water in seaports was always a problem. Few people realize that up until relatively recently Amsterdam was situated on the coast and that at ebb-tide, Amsterdam wormers and cocklers used to take their sleighs to the mud flats near Diemerzeedijk (to the east of the city).

In this saline and brackish environment, the river Amstel was of course a source of fresh water, but the latter was unsafe because of the tanneries and tar yards situated upstream. In dry periods, drinking water was shipped in. Virtually all of the canalside houses in Amsterdam were adapted to the economical use of rainwater; to this end, for example, they were equipped with water basements and glazed roof tiles. Nevertheless, this water was often undrinkable because of bacterial contamination, and in effect this is how Dutch beer came into being. Nowadays, a glass of beer with breakfast is perhaps considered a bit unusual, but brewing beer is of course a way of processing water in order to preserve it.

When Amsterdammers leave their city's sphere of influence, they envelope themselves in an aura of metropolitan overconfidence, or are seized by a strong sense of oppression. Both emotions are due to the strong attachment Amsterdammers feel for their city, and to their proverbial chauvinism. Newcomers to the city, who have only recently exchanged Paramaribo (Surinam) or some remote corner of the Netherlands for Amsterdam, display similar behaviour. This takes place within such a short space of time that there must be some agent producing this change of attitude.

My theory, which has yet to be contradicted, is that this phenomenon has everything to do with the addictive properties of Amsterdam's drinking-water. This water is of a very high quality, delicious, and available to everyone. The city council provides it free of charge to every thirsty passer-by, via the beautiful cast-iron drinking fountains along the public highway. The distinctive taste (neutral, refreshing, yet slightly creamy and full-bodied) is due to a combination of types of water. The secret lies in mixing water from two different sources.

One quarter of this mixture is drawn from the 25 million cubic metres of water obtained annually from the Bethune polder. A large amount of seepage water rises in this small polder (situated four metres below sea level) from a deep groundwater stream which flows from the neighbouring Utrecht ridge. This water has been on its way for hundreds of years and has picked up all manner of minerals and trace elements along its subterranean course. As regards ionic composition (and thus taste) it has a pronounced lithotrophic character.

The remaining three quarters is dune water. Beneath the coastal dunes – literally floating on the deeper saline groundwater – is a large 'bubble' of fresh water. This is rainwater which has seeped down through the sand layer and is free of bacteria because of the low temperature at this great depth. This source has been used to produce Amsterdam's drinking-water since 1854. Because catchment began to exceed the annual precipitation surplus, since 1957 purified river water has been infiltrated in the dunes. The total amount of water with a more atmotrophic character thus obtained amounts to some 70 million cubic metres. If this combination

had not come into being more or less by accident, we would, like the Scottish, be able to speak of a successful 'blend' of various 'malts'. The flavour is so distinctive that the really advanced metropolis-spotter would immediately be able to identify Amsterdam tap water in a blind taste test.

What measures need to be taken in order to safeguard this flow of precious liquid in the future (even if demand rises sharply), if at the same time consideration has to be given to reducing the detrimental ecological effects (drying up of sources, for example) of water catchment? In the first place, there are plans to obtain a larger proportion of Amsterdam's production in the dunes. This would involve the use of a new technique, the so-called deep-infiltration technique, whereby the river water no longer filters from ground level in the arenaceous dune floor, but is introduced in deep fall pipes at a depth of 25 metres. The advantage of this method is that the characteristic dune vegetation does not absorb nutriments which are present in large quantities in the river water.

There are also plans for the other source of water in the Utrecht ridge. Under consideration at the moment is the possibility of discontinuing groundwater catchment here. Catchment would be resumed only when the water has done its beneficial work for nature in the form of seepage. It ought to be possible to store water obtained in the wet season in the ground profile or in specially constructed surface basins. Large tracts of the area will as a result be less suitable for agriculture, but

Drinking fountain

the plus-point of this solution is that it is sustainable; sustainable in the sense that the amount of water collected does not exceed that which falls in the entire catchment basin in precipitation surplus. A requirement is that the water companies purchase land and that large parts of the Vecht lake district become nature reserves.

The cost of these plans could be covered by a rise in the price of water of approximately 30 cents per cubic metre. And the inhabitants of Amsterdam, the city of Utrecht and the region in between (Het Gooi) would have an enormous nature reserve and recreation area providing them with water for bathing, showering, washing the car, washing-up, etcetera. It means that – together with the reserve function the IJmeer and Markermeer (large lakes to the east and north-east of Amsterdam) are to fulfil for the production of drinking-water for the entire Western Netherlands – in the future, Amsterdam will be surrounded by large areas with a function for drinking-water production. And then the connection between the minuscule urban element of the water mains cover and the largest 'detail' becomes clear: the urban configuration – the location and the city form which determine whether inhabitants of the city feel confined or not.

Because of the diffuse distribution of building development and the complex interrelationships between the component cities and towns, the Amsterdam agglomeration (which forms the northern wing of the Randstad, the urban agglomeration of Western Holland) is in danger of filling up and becoming one large nondescript urbanized area. There is a pressing need therefore for a strategic link between drinking-water catchment, nature conservation and the recreational requirements of city dwellers.

The commitment to these three social concerns could result in the new and old catchment areas becoming the most important open areas in the carpet metropolis which is now unrolling. New wildernesses would be created near Amsterdam, which because of their informal and public character would be 'wildernesses to lose oneself in', and which, because of their size and allure, could serve as a counterpoint to the well-regulated urban household agenda.

The anticipated sharp rise in the price of drinking-water on the world market will ensure that these investments are recovered. If the price of water around the year 2030 approximates that of crude oil (as the United Nations forecasts), than that delicious Amsterdam delicacy will not only be more addictive, but also more expensive than that other speciality for which the city is famous, the soft drugs.

Zooming in and out · Theoretically, our man-made landscape (read: city) is a collection of individual expressions (read: architecture), linked by means of a common complex of agreements and regulations (read: urbanism).

The architectural detail is the terminus of the operation of a concept. In that sense, for the viewer, the concept reverberates in the detail and vice versa. It is a process of zooming swiftly in and out.

The architectural detail in the city, glimpsed by the passer-by, is the ultimate invitation to probe – a sign that somewhere more is going on than the surface, that there is depth.

CRAFT ARCHITECTURE
HENK ZANTKUIJL

One of the characteristics of Amsterdam's historic city centre is the craft architecture of the street façades which, in a fascinating and expressive way, enclose the public space. This architecture's great power of expression is partly due to the meticulous masonry and the careful application of wood and stone, the sole function of which is to enrich the street. The expressive detailing of the functional and constructional elements plays a key role. An important aspect is that, because of the way in which the elements (for example, the door, door frame or gable cornice) are assembled to form a whole, both the whole and all of the component parts receive due attention.

We are able to 'read' this detailing because there is light and therefore shadow. Consequently, the form of the detailing is designed to catch light. Convex and concave surfaces intensify the light into sharp lines of light and soft shadows, while the straight edges in between produce hard shadows. The way in which these effects of light and shadow are orchestrated tells us in which period the detail was given its expressive form.

The most striking sections of the street façades, in which this meticulous detailing shows to best advantage, are the lower façade at eye-level and the termination of the façade against the sky. The lower façade is the immediate boundary of the public space at street level and has a direct influence on the experiential value of this space. The upper termination of the façade marks the point where material (finiteness) and universe (infinity) flow into one another. This latter area for attention has always played an important role in historical architecture, namely as a means of giving a building an autonomous character within the unity of the street façade, and of showing this to best advantage. Let us look more closely at both areas for attention and their detailing.

Entablature · The mode of detailing in the major architectural periods after the Renaissance is largely derived from the various elements of the characteristic entablature of Greek and Roman architecture. This entablature (known popularly as the cornice) is essentially a functional drip to keep rain from the façade below. The need for this protection and the way in which it took shape has meant that the cornice has survived throughout the centuries.

The many variations of the detailing of the entablature are all based on one basic principle (see illustration on p. 61, in which this basic idea of an entablature is executed as a gable cornice). The uppermost, projecting section is called the cornice. The straight section below the convex moulding (the so-called echinus)

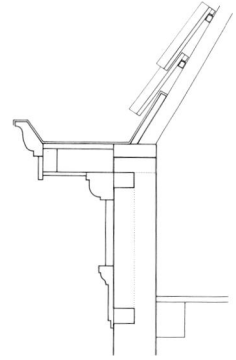

*Basic
principle of
entablature*

is referred to as the frieze. The lowest element, the original beam resting on the columns of Greek and Roman temple fronts, is called the architrave. The various profiles of these details can be found in the treatises of the Renaissance architects Serlio, Vignola, Palladio and Scamozzi.

An interesting variant is the entablature used in the girls' court of the former Burgerweeshuis (city orphanage, now the Amsterdam Historical Museum). It was built between 1632 and 1635 to a design by Jacob van Campen, who followed Scamozzi's treatise here (see illustrations on pp. 62-63). The cornice projects on consoles (the small beams which support the gutter bottom). The strongly convex mouldings of this section, which is executed entirely in wood, increase its allure.

The frieze is of brick, the architrave is of sandstone. The photograph shows how the architrave relates to the corners of the window frames. The joint between

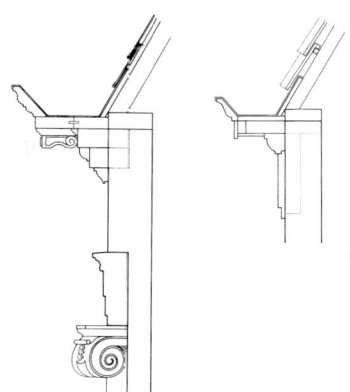

◄
*Burgerwees-
huis* [Jacob
van Campen,
1635]

*Entablature
of Burger-
weeshuis*

*Basic
principle of
abbreviated
entablature*

the masonry and the wood of the window frames is covered with a board whose detailing follows the form of the architrave. This correspondence between the mouldings of the architrave and the cover board is a centuries-old practice.

Seventeenth-century classicism was not the only style to use the architrave as a window frame. Later architectural styles which were based on classicism also made use of this detail. This can be seen, for example, in the theatre the Kleine Komedie on the Amstel (Abraham van der Hart, 1785), and in the former Willemspoort – now Haarlemmerpoort – on Haarlemmerplein completed in 1840 to a design by C. Alewijn and C.W.M. Klijn.

The classical architrave is bounded by a sharp line. In the Baroque, this straight line was often replaced by a convex moulding which produces a line of light as a boundary (see p. 67). As the drawing shows, in the Baroque and Rococo there were many variations.

Hoog Duitse Synagogue
[Elias Bouman, 1670]

The most detailed variants were primarily used in the interior. Because the architrave model has a pronounced framing character, traditional picture frames are largely based on them and this gave rise to the most fanciful variants.

Abbreviated entablature · A variant of the original entablature is the abbreviated model. It was often used after 1620 (see p. 63) and is known popularly as the abbreviated cornice. In addition to being used to crown façades, it was also employed for the detailing of gutters and side walls. Because of its perfect gutter form, it continued to be used up until the beginning of this century. As a termination of a façade, it is chiefly to be found in sober government buildings and public buildings. Examples are the former Hoog Duitse Synagogue on Nieuwe Amstelstraat (now the Jewish Historical Museum), built in 1670 to a design by Elias Bouman, the Portugees Israëlitische Synagogue in the square

Baroque entablature

Mr Visserplein (Elias Bouman, 1671) and the church Oosterkerk on Wittenburgergracht (Daniël Stalpaert, 1669).

In the eighteenth century, the taut form of the classical entablature was altered. Its basic cross-section remained much the same, but the cornice was broken and/or bent upwards in the middle. This deformation, which was often accompanied by an additional Baroque ornament, gave the façade a strong central accent.

Hoisting beam · A highly characteristic Amsterdam façade detail, which, in a functional way, often provides a central accent, is the hoisting beam. It is essentially a rectangular beam which on the inside is attached to the roof construction, and on the outside is equipped with a hoisting hook. The transverse section shows how the beam, which projects from the façade, is protected from the rain and decay by a small roof

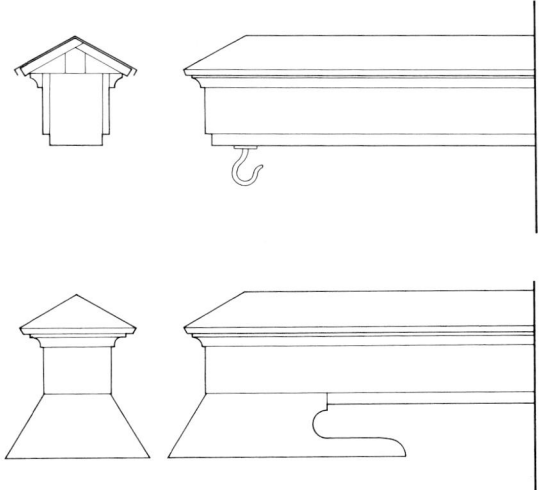

*Hoisting
beams
(below:
with locking
planks)*

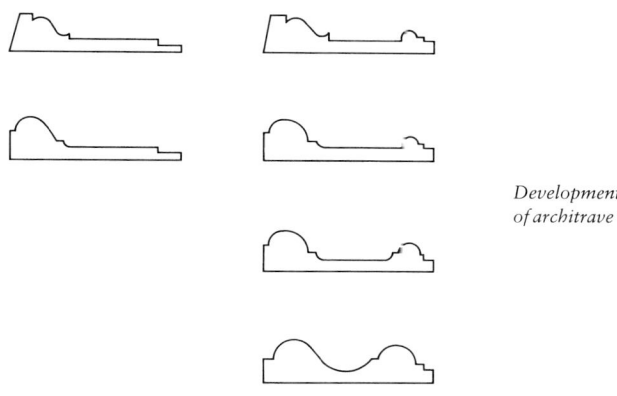

*Development
of architrave*

covered with lead. The joint between the small roof and
the beam is stopped by means of an ogee moulding. The
underside is accentuated by creating a shadow surface
with a plank or a slat, as a starting point for a termination on the underside. Sometimes, locking planks are
fitted into the groove on the underside in order to prevent the pulley from being pulled off the hook during
hoisting and, with their characteristic shape, give an
additional accent to the hoisting beam.

Coping moulding and transoms · The abbreviated
cornice is the basis of a detail which is applied in many
ways. The lowermost section is to be found in the form
of coping mouldings and transoms. With one peculiar-
ity: in contrast to the architrave, which is applied (and
viewed) both vertically and horizontally, this moulding
is only used horizontally and in situations in which it is
viewed from below. This fact is exploited in countless
ways (see p. 68).

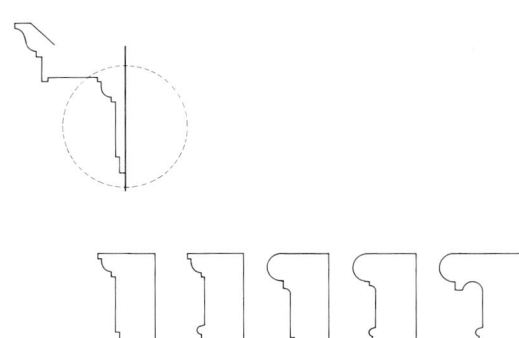

Development of abbreviated cornice

Here too, the underside usually has a true termination. This is as a rule due to a groove which accentuates the sharp bounding line on the underside by means of an additional shadow surface. If a convex moulding is used, then the effect of the shadow surface is reinforced by a line of light. In the Baroque, the sharp line on the top of the cornice is also replaced by a convex moulding with a line of light as a boundary. The development of the moulding up until the Baroque resembles that of the architrave (see p. 67).

Lower façade · Obviously, with the exception of the upper termination, the most important façade details are situated where they can best be seen: on the lower section of the façade, usually on the door and door frames. Take, for example, the upper section of the door of 476 Herengracht (see opposite page).

A door of this type consists of jambs, sills and lintels which enclose panels. The joints between the panel and

the jambs and sills and lintels are stopped by means of cover boards and cover mouldings. Their form is derived from the architrave (see p. 67), but is considerably shortened. Thus, the fillet not only covers the joint, but also frames the panel and clarifies its size and proportions. A striking characteristic of Baroque detailing of a panel construction is that the right angle is sometimes wholly or partly negated, and in that case is replaced by curved forms. The mouldings on the panel itself have no constructional function and merely serve to give additional emphasis to the panel's size and proportions.

The door is painted a single colour (dark green). The convex and concave mouldings produce lines of light which clearly differentiate the various elements. The transom (between the door and the transom window) has the profile of the abbreviated cornice (see p. 68, on the far right) and is moreover embellished with acanthus leaves.

Bead mouldings · Door and window frames have for centuries been given an additional boundary by means of convex mouldings. The so-called bead moulding has been popular since the eighteenth century. This bead moulding (one of the oldest accentuations in Dutch architecture) is a round stick placed on the inside corner of the frame (see p. 71 above, on the left). It gives the frame's inner surface an additional line of light. Technically, the stick can form part of the wood of the frame, but can also be one of the parts of which the frame is composed, because with bead moulding the joint is carefully concealed (p. 71 above, on the right). This facilitated the conversion of the seventeenth-

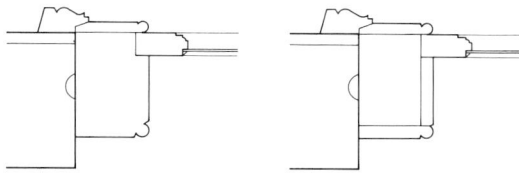

*Window
with bead
moulding*

*Front door of
Nederlandsche
Bank
[W.A. Froger,
1869]*

century cross-bar window into the eighteenth-century sash window. The lintel and mullion were simply removed.

A combination of bead moulding and coping moulding can be seen on the front door of the former Nederlandsche Bank (now the Allard Pierson Museum) by W.A. Froger (1869). The panels are surrounded by bead moulding (see p. 71 below). Cast-iron grilles have been fitted in the panels, which are held in place by mouldings in the form of abbreviated architraves. Because the architecture of the building has all the features of mid-nineteenth-century classicism, the mouldings are bounded by straight lines.

Sometimes the jambs of the wooden lower façade, near the door and near the windows, are accentuated by means of bead mouldings. In that case, the panels of the lower and upper door are held in place by cover boards with strongly convex mouldings (Baroque). Consequently, as was customary in the Baroque and Rococo, they lack the right-angle solutions. The cordon (the string course above the basement) has an eighteenth-century moulding, derived from the abbreviated cornice (see p. 68, second from the right). The termination on the top has an illuminated convex moulding which is characteristic of the period in which it was made. The lintel between the door and the transom window is a somewhat more traditional variant with a straight top line and an ogee as a moulding to catch the light.

Entrance steps · Finally, in order to show how functional the details of Amsterdam entrance steps are, let us take a look at the entrance of 312 Herengracht (see

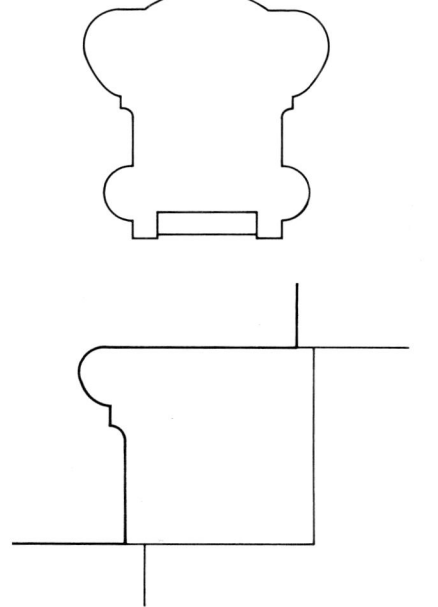

Banister (above) and entrance step (below)

p. 73 below and p. 74). The detail of the steps is derived from the abbreviated cornice (p. 68). As the steps are situated below eye level, there was no point in accentuating the underside. The pronounced convexity on the top means that light is caught even at dusk, so that the steps and the slab can be distinguished.

The balusters and the banisters are also moulded in this way. The cross-section of the banister not only provides an excellent handrail, but also ensures that the banister is clearly distinguishable because of the lines of light (see p. 73 above). Here too, the abbreviated cornice moulding has been used. The centre bar between the balusters is usually rounded and thus gives a good line of light. At 312 Herengracht, the bar is twisted, as a result of which a pearl line attracts attention (a technique copied from goldsmiths and silversmiths).

What all the details described here have in common is that they are orientated towards the street, and are therefore shaped so that they are readable from the street. They bear witness to the great care and devotion with which in past centuries the walls of the public space were designed and detailed, and, despite their simplicity, give extra lustre, an extra dimension, to the architecture of Amsterdam's fascinating centre.

312 Herengracht

PETER ELLIS

URBAN DETAIL

FROM A BRICK TO A CITY
FROM ONE PIECE TO A WHOLE
A UNITY OF PARTS IN ENDLESS VARIATION
THE BRICK IS THE BEGINNING OF
    ARCHITECTURE
THE PRIMARY DETAIL OF THE CITY

THE BRICK MAKES A WALL
THE GENIUS OF AMSTERDAM IS THAT THE
    WALL BECOMES A FRAME
THE FRAME CREATES A VOID
THE VOID IS SHEATHED IN WHITE LACE
A TRANSPARANT LATTICE WITH INFINITE
    VARIATION
FINE, DELICATE, OPEN, CLOSED, WIDE, THIN
AN ENDLESS FUGUE OF FRAME AND LIGHT TO
    ANIMATE THIS BEAUTIFUL CITY

CUYPERS' GARDEN GATE

AART OXENAAR

'No money, no detail, only pure concept.' This maxim of Rem Koolhaas' is prompted by a pragmatic approach to the modern building practice, in which the market and the construction budget hold the architect in an iron grip. This is of course only natural. But at the same time, it is nothing less than a contemporary version of the age-old Dutch principle of frugality, a principle which runs like a leitmotif through Dutch architectural history.

Frugality, not in the sense of penny-pinching and small-mindedness, nor as the hypocritical exterior for 'the embarrassment of riches' (which is how the historian Simon Schama characterizes Dutch seventeenth-century culture), but frugality in the standard sense of an efficient and economical use of resources as a basis for a healthy architectural language. I deliberately use the word 'healthy', because since it erupted round about the middle of the last century, the stylistic debate in the Netherlands has been permeated with political, ideological and socio-therapeutic pretensions: 'Show me your details and I shall tell you who you are'.

Handwriting · In the eyes of the Catholic architect P.J.H. Cuypers, an excess of detail was sinful; in the eyes of the social democrat H.P. Berlage, it was a false guide along the road to utopia; in the eyes of J. Duiker and comrades, it was anti-social; for the members of the Dutch architects' group Forum (Aldo van Eyck, Herman Hertzberger and others), it was an impediment to the development of the group process. Finally, in the case of Koolhaas, detail does not even get a look-in. But ornament or detail was and is in all their work – even Koolhaas' non-detail produces a recognizable handwriting; and in all their work, detail played and plays a significant role.

This is the second leitmotif in Dutch architectural history: architecture as the expression of an idea. Anyone who looks at the building production will observe that in the Netherlands, too, autonomous architecture has played an important role. But the debate and historiography are dominated by the avant-garde and its perennial claims that it has found the only true mode of expression for the ideal society. Ornament, the detail, plays a central role in this quest.

Already in the nineteenth century, architectural theory made a distinction between style in construction and style in ornament. Developments in construction followed developments in science and technology. Construction was also dependent on the economic situation and derived its 'style' from it. Ornament, on the

Garden gate [P.J.H. Cuypers, 1881]

other hand, was the personal handwriting with which the artist/architect could elevate the banal building into an expressive work of art. By means of ornament, a structure could be elevated into the expression of an idea, building became *gemeenschapskunst* ('communal art'). In short, ornament embodied the building's message. And – in spite of Koolhaas' dictum – this is what it still is. Ornament as the recognizable decorative addition to the structure, it is true, gradually disappeared, but the detailing of the structure itself took over its role. A tour of those architectural high points in Amsterdam which history has elevated into anchor points in the progressive development of architecture soon makes this clear.

Berlage and Cuypers · H.P. Berlage was one of the architects who constructed this genealogy of progressive buildings. The avant-garde had and still has a need for an ancestry, and as if to strengthen its history and the sense of family appropriate to this self-constructed project of the modern, Berlage traced his link with the father of Dutch modern architecture back to his childhood years. As a young boy, Hendrik Pieter lived in Vondelstraat in Amsterdam, and he recalled how visitors to his parents' house often admired the decorations on the garden gate next door. This was not just any neighbour, and not just any old gate. The neighbour was P.J.H. Cuypers, leading light of the progressive neo-Gothic movement in the Netherlands, and the garden gate was a piece of ornamental ironwork produced in the latter's own workshops. In this detail, years later, Berlage discovered the connection with his own innovative work.

*Centraal
Station*
[P.J.H.
Cuypers,
1889]

P.J.H. Cuypers was one of the first architects in the Netherlands to employ ornament in a personal and ideological way in order to save architecture as a social art. By embellishing a modern, rational structure with ornament inspired by the Middle Ages, Cuypers believed he would be able to give contemporary buildings the same signification as his great example, the masterpiece of Gothic: the cathedral. One glance at Cuypers' Amsterdam *oeuvre* – the Rijksmuseum (1885), Centraal Station (1889), three churches and a residential street (Vondelstraat) – reveals how ornament is always deployed in order to clarify the structure and, at the same time, in order to give it a symbolic added value. The corner chains along the central towers of the Rijksmuseum and Centraal Station are characteristic of Cuypers' use of detail. The masonry of a tower is lighter towards the top, and Cuypers shows this by means of a corner chain which is heavily bossed at the level of the basement and first articulation, flat along

Rijksmuseum
[P.J.H.
Cuypers,
1885]

the second articulation and becomes a slender colonnet on the third tower articulation.

The structure is thus readable in the façade, but for Cuypers it is also an occasion to let the stones speak by means of ornament. The dictum 'unity in diversity', often propagated in nineteenth-century architectural theory, is given an ideological import here. The building as a readable stacking of various materials and a recognizable composition composed of different programmatic elements is also a prefiguration of a society composed of many parts. It reflects Cuypers' ideal of a corporative society. This, too, was built from the bottom up, in imitation of the old guilds. Sculptures, reliefs, tile pictures and stained-glass windows on the façade elucidate the building's message to anyone who takes the trouble to read this complex programme.

Imagery · Berlage admired the 'rationality' of Cuypers' structures but did not care for the explicit

Christian-corporatist content of his imagery. Although the handling of the façade of the Rijksmuseum and Centraal Station was austere for the time, in Berlage's view Cuypers' ornamentation was too elaborate and thus out of keeping with the poor state of the country's economy. In Cuypers' view, ornamentation should reflect the importance of a building. Berlage was far more radical. According to the latter, even an important public building should not ignore the economic reality. His Beurs (Exchange, 1903), erected in the heart of Amsterdam, opposite Centraal Station, was thus a stern response to Cuypers' work. The façades of the Beurs have been stretched like a taut skin around the skeleton, and ornament is limited to decorations in the flat surface. Openings in the wall – galleries, window openings, door frames – look as if they have been cut out the surface with a sharp knife. For constructional reasons, these have been strengthened with stone, but even the decoration of this stonework remains within the façade surface.

This restraint in the use of ornament also had to do with Berlage's vision of the future. With his neo-Gothic *Gesamtkunstwerk*, Cuypers gave an almost literal prefiguration of his ideal society. According to Berlage, it was impossible to know precisely what the future society would look like. The architect could merely give an overall impression. The corner turret on the north side of the Beurs, directly opposite the richly decorated entrance to Centraal Station, typifies the differences between the two architects: a flat façade, severe and clean-cut arches and on the acute corner a sculpted figure which remains within the façade surface. Berlage made use of an elaborate iconographic programme in

order to elevate his building into communal art. But the most pregnant detail of his building is its silhouette. The building as a whole evokes an image of the late-medieval Italian city-states, Berlage's ideal of a democratic urban community.

White boxes · Many of Berlage's contemporaries considered the Beurs to be incomplete. What was lacking, in their view, was the 'finish of the work': the ornamentation. In the view of the next generation of architects, however, Berlage had not gone far enough. Duiker's Openluchtschool (Open Air School, 1930) in Cliostraat is the next step in the progression of avant-garde architecture in Amsterdam. And when the white boxes with flat roofs and steel windows were proclaimed the materials of the new Jerusalem, now with a social democratic flavour, ornament was dispensed with altogether. Light, air and green space were the new requirements, and the new architecture seemed to spring naturally out of the practical, sound and economically feasible solution to this sanitary programme. In order to create as much space as possible, and to give people maximum freedom in the space, the building had to be 'dematerialized'. It had, as it were, to efface itself. The architect appeared to withdraw in order to address himself to the efficient organization of the programme and the translation of this into a structure.

The recent problems with the restoration of the country's modernist heritage, however, underline just how important detail was for the modernists. Slight changes in the detailing of concrete structures, edges of

Beurs, north façade [H.P. Berlage, 1903]

Column of light and air, Openlucht-school [J. Duiker, 1930]

roofs, window profiles and window tracery, or minor alterations to connecting details can alter the character of the building to such an extent that the intention of the architect is blotted out. Thin and slender were the watchwords of the modernists as regards detailing. Frugality was elevated into an absolute virtue.

Characteristic of the modernist approach is the corner detail of the Openluchtschool. With an eye to the spatial effect in the classrooms, Duiker omitted the support here. Thanks to the modern concrete-framed construction, this did not present a structural problem. But by setting the glass façades on this 'open' corner back slightly, Duiker nevertheless suggested a corner column, a column of light and air. A more symbolically charged response to Cuypers' solid corner chains and the heavy towers on the corners of the Beurs is scarcely conceivable. With this detail, the classical orders of columns literally evaporated into thin air. The ornament was 'dematerialized', although it did not disappear.

Industrial reproduction · Standardization was a central concern of the modernists. Traditional methods of building were outmoded and attention focused on the efficient industrial reproduction of well-designed standard components. Man could then apply his creativity to higher things. After the war, this pragmatic side of modernism proved to be a perfect vehicle for the rapid standardization and industrialization of house-building, which was vital in order to ease the country's housing shortage. However, in so doing modernism also turned against itself and criticism very soon erupted. The new building for the Amsterdam Burgerwees-huis (Orphanage) by Van Eyck – the next step in the genealogy of the avant-garde in Amsterdam – became the icon of a generation of critical young modernists.

As a reaction to the anonymous uniformity of standardized mass-produced housing, these architects went in search of new forms to give meaningful expression to an open society. The monumentality of the building was renounced and was replaced by a flexible structure of spatial units, which could be linked to form larger units, according to need or the programme. The central concern was not the space itself, but the way in which space was provided in the building for a mode of living or working together.

Paradoxically, in Van Eyck's Weeshuis this led to the revival of a classical detail: column and entablature, support and beam. Where Duiker created openness by omitting supports, Van Eyck created the freedom to link spaces by means of a simple and flexible constructional system of supports and beams. Column and beam thus became far more than just a constructional detail. They embodied Van Eyck's attempts to redefine

*Burger-
weeshuis*
[Aldo van
Eyck, 1960]

*Oriel of
Byzantium*
[Rem
Koolhaas
(OMA),
1991]

the relationship between the individual and the community. At another level, too, ornament returned in Van Eyck's work: as a whimsical addition to the building. Coloured tiles, mirrors, colourful glass strips invite users to touch, to look at themselves in, to play with the building.

The Weeshuis attests to Van Eyck's belief in the possibility of interweaving private and public, architecture and city. Rem Koolhaas' apartment block Byzantium, situated between Vondelpark and Vondelstraat – the end point, for the time being, in the evolution of the avant-garde in Amsterdam – has heavy-handedly put an end to this idyll. Van Eyck's subtle staging of a congenial environment has made way for market-oriented scenarios for steering the rapidly changing metropolis. The building is merely a set piece, a shell for the efficient stacking of urban functions. Details are only present if that is what the market demands.

In Byzantium, a canopy, which penetrates deep into the building, increases the allure of the luxury shops on the ground floor. The kidney-shaped oriel on the corner of the building, intended as a restaurant with views of the city, was built at the request of a software manufacturer: as a living-room. The detail says nothing meaningful about the city, but merely represents its reality. The economy, now in the sense of the operation of the market, has of necessity been elevated here into an ideal. The banal gold colour of the postmodern oriel underlines this, and at the same time is a critical comment on it. Koolhaas submits to the operation of the market, but this is not to say that he accepts it.

From Byzantium to Cuypers' garden gate is not only a few steps as the crow flies.

Shelters for traffic wardens · Recently, after careful consideration, we declined the commission to make a study of suitable accommodation for traffic wardens and produce a design concept.

The commission started us thinking about the city, that is, about the concept of the city in general, about Amsterdam in particular and, especially, about the degree of spatial tolerance a city needs in order to be a true city. This line of thought also included the role of urban planning.

We notice daily that the role of the supervisory urbanist is increasingly being limited to control over the use of materials, the quality of land division, the position of refuse containers and choice of paving stone. Real spatial decisions are made at an earlier stage by the development company, developers and (local) politicians, in conformity with the needs of the market.

This development means that the urban public space, important though it is, is becoming the object of an excess of design, not out of necessity but out of frustration.

We have come to the conclusion that a conceptual approach, given the solution sought (in this case by the client), is undesirable. At the same time, we do not consider ourselves capable of optimizing designs for standard accommodation for the traffic wardens, since we prefer the imperfection of the makeshift shacks, which at the present moment are a blot on the cityscape, to a perfectly detailed Ford cabin.

FUNCTIONS OF THE DETAIL

BEN VAN BERKEL & CAROLINE BOS

Contemporary architecture seems to be unfolding, both inside and outside, according to some universal plot. This alienating effect is exacerbated by the severance of every link between what takes place inside a building and what can be seen of this from the outside. Because of this development, it has become essential to redefine the significance of the detail. Its classical role, as a part of the whole, as articulation, has become obsolete.

The idea of ornamentation had long been discarded, but now even the notion of articulation has been abandoned. What is there to articulate in today's architecture when it can be entered using every kind of technique, and whose entrance therefore need be no more monumental than a power point? Neither its structure nor its place in its surroundings says anything about a building's purpose.

This is why detail has ended up in a black hole; architecture questions its ability to exist. In response to the

Offices and storages, Generaal Vetterstraat [Mart Stam, 1961]

need to find new ways of applying detail, we propose 'Four Functions of the Detail'. Four circuitous and furtive routes for redefining detail in its disconnected state, which together encapsulate how structures are changing today; they are losing their specific, separate properties and are defined increasingly by the way in which they relate to the organization of the whole and how users of architecture are related to them.

First Function · The first Function of the Detail is that of omission; the significance of detail for architecture under present-day conditions is more likely to reside in the opposite of a well-placed column, a refined edge or an elaborate corner than in instances of unleashed and unhooked articulation. Instead of being concerned with underlining, emphasizing, paraphrasing, this detail is solely a matter of leaving out. It is a detail which consists of an absence, a conscious discarding of superfluous articulation.

Second Function · The second Function of the Detail is that of the imaginary extension. This principle is founded on the extension of lines glimpsed out of the corner of the eye, the unfurling of accidental pockets of residual space in corners of the site, and the dredging up of parallels with half-hidden substrata. Although this second Function of the Detail can be incorporated as a component part of the building, the detail as imaginary extension is in essence scale-less. This detail has a tendency to absorb the main structure; the new detail has no self-evident scale, no prescribed size, no limitation with regard to its relative proportioning.

This approach to detail implies a new way of positioning architecture in the environment and fixing it there without quotation, or formulation; not to provide an explanation, but to experience with the senses.

Third Function · The third Function of the Detail is that of finding; finding and storing the detail that is already there. The architecture follows the finds, wraps itself around them and opens itself up again to display its found origins.

This description suggests a retiring attitude, an architecture which almost passively awaits, submits, withdraws – never asserts; and this is indeed partly the case. Yet this reticence must not be overestimated; there is always a selection, which necessarily contains traces of brutality and the presentation of discreet segments also implies a mutilation, a corruption. What is more, the stored detail is interpreted differently out of its ori-ginal setting; the presence of the found detail has become a memory of the sundering, of the process of change, rather than a memory of the past. This process

*City centre-project,
De Kolk*
[Van Berkel
& Bos, 1996]

*Housing,
Plantage
Parklaan*
[Meyer
& Van
Schooten,
1988]
➤

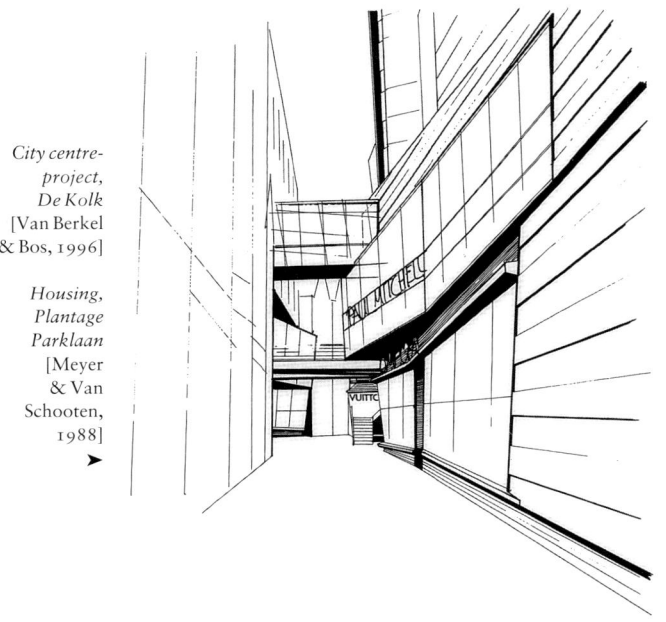

Waterloo-
plein
[W. Holz-
bauer,
C. Dam,
B. Bijvoet,
1987]

is more interesting and more meaningful than the bloodless and sentimental nostalgia for an imagined history, the distortions of the past of which architecture is also guilty.

Transferred to the urban level, the iniquities inherent in the seeming passiveness of finding become even more apparent. Our project for the centre of Amsterdam, De Kolk, demonstrates how unrelated to scale this detail is in its application. Here, the found detail pertains to the totality of the urban structure, in which entire housing blocks disappear and are stored, enveloped by a new system, which is perhaps comparable to a skin, although this is a morphological metaphor which is used too often and always misleads.

The only aspect of this system that invites comparison with skin is its layered nature and the unpleasantness of its tearing, rather than its suggestion of extreme thinness. The urban pain of pushing and pulling at wounds is not denied, pathetic though this may sound;

the stored detail, as a strange souvenir, at once *memento mori* and living memory, brings some consolation in this unremitting process.

Fourth Function · The fourth Function of the Detail relates to a new way of structuring to replace classical composition. As a detail, it is both beginning and end, a detail extended to exclude everything else. New structures take the place of architectural compositions composed of separate details. These new architectural structures resemble scientifically determined 'dissipative structures', open, evolving systems, in the same way in which an urban static structure can be said to be an open system of energy incorporating economic, social and political information.

Structures actually amount to process fields of materializations, based on spatial shifting devices, rather than representing any homogeneous, linear system. This allows for a completely different idea of urban typology, both as an understanding of our contemporary reality and as an organizational system. Being more inclusive of social morphologies and physical organizational processes, it contains a multiplicity of dimensions and directions.

Integration · Elaborate details in a townscape serve to enrich buildings. The city as a man-made piece of art requires an overlapping of readings at different scales.

Among urban design strategies, the goodness in urban morphology provides an excellent 'liaison' between urbanistic and architectural qualities.

Precisely when the topography is difficult, urban layout can integrate the right scale of outdoor space with the grain of the buildings.

DUMB DETAILS

GORDON HASLETT

Balconies · Balconies are required for all new dwellings in Amsterdam, in order to house the 'bio bak' (see below and illustration on p. 106, below). The balcony rail usually consists of vertical metal bars; horizontal bars are not allowed for safety reasons. Many people weave plastic sheets through the metal bars in order to reduce wind and increase privacy when sitting on their balcony. The balcony rail is always the same height, again for safety reasons, so the plastic sheets can be made in standard sizes.

Basketball · Asphalt courts are provided throughout the city. The supports for the baskets are similar in shape, but the detail varies. It is strange how even such specific elements of the city don't always look exactly the same.

Bicycle racks · As is the case with parking spaces, there are never enough. Often, the galvanized metal

loop provided for the lock has been forced open with a crowbar. The violence embodied in the broken loop is worrying evidence of another, unseen world of gangs of thieves and junkies.

Bio bak · These are bright green garbage cans designed specifically for domestic biodegradable material. They are placed on the pavement for joint collection, so the traditional streets get a taste of bright, shiny, new, colourful modernity at least one morning every week.

Boardroom · The Nissan building is located just outside Amsterdam's main ring road. Projecting from an upper floor of the slender slab is a small, curved, glazed volume containing the boardroom. From inside this elevated room, the decision-makers can look out across their European market. Rarely is the strategy 'form follows function' applied so precisely and so romantically.

Dog shit · The most powerful and repulsive urban detail of all, and Amsterdam is full of it. Its effect is to force Amsterdammers into a constant and thorough study of the ground plane; looking up for extended periods is hazardous. The relief of being able to look up in other cities adds to their glamour.

Hoisting beams · Part of the iconography of the canalside house, they enable goods to be moved in and out using a rope and pulley. Moving house in this way provides a rare opportunity for maximum public display of personal possessions.

Mirrors · Car wing mirrors are attached to the façades of some canalside houses. From inside, the mirror provides a view down to the front door. Unlike the modern door phone, this system enables you to choose whether to 'be in' or not, depending on who the caller is. The blunt attachment of a car part to a sixteenth-century canalside house relieves the 'suspended animation' character of the inner canals.

Noise screens · Amsterdam's northern ring road is six lanes wide. On either side, silver aluminium screens gracefully curve up from the road to a height of about four metres. The screens deflect road noise into the air and away from neighbouring housing development. Driving between these walls of silver aluminium along the perfectly maintained black asphalt at 140 kilometres per hour is a truly 'James Bond experience'. Of course, speed cameras ensure that such experiences are paid for.

Orange flags · To make children's bikes safer, long flexible sticks with orange flags on top are attached to them. The expression 'Oranje boven' (orange on top) refers to a narrow orange strip flown above the Dutch flag, indicating allegiance to the House of Orange. So the dual themes of safety and politics converge on children's bikes throughout Amsterdam and the Netherlands – accurately reflecting the two corner-stones of current city planning.

Parking meters · Pay-parking is a major growth industry in Amsterdam. The parking meters are rede-signed with each new wave of pay-parking coloniza-tion of larger and larger parts of the city. The new meters enable you to pay in the evening for parking the following morning. This means that it is no longer necessary to get up early to 'feed the meter'. If you choose not to pay, your car will be wheel-clamped (see below). In order to pay for the removal of the clamp you have to visit the traffic police, who thank you for your custom and dispatch a clamp-removal crew.

Pavement tiles · Pavements in the inner city are always too narrow; in the inner city, everything is too narrow. In the surrounding neighbourhoods, pave-ments are made from the same, small concrete tiles. However, these tiles may vary. Rubber tiles are used in children's play areas. Graphic tiles indicate where to place rubbish bags for collection. Bumps on the tile sur-face help blind people to locate zebra crossings. Tiles with images of a squatting dog and an arrow remind dog owners not to let their pets foul the pavement, and that the gutter should be used instead.

Pissoir · These are just like the ones in Paris, but are under-used (see illustration on p. 133). At any time of day or night, men prefer to urinate directly into the canal. This seems odd, yet no one appears to be particularly concerned.

Public art · In Amsterdam, public art is widespread, never radical, but always slightly confusing.

Recycling containers · Clear glass, green glass, paper, clothing – each has its own specially designed recycling container. In Amsterdam, this is an emerging technology. Some containers are small, some large, some underground, with different colours, differrent forms. The differences between the types seem to increase their number and their dominance in the street.

Red lights · Amsterdam's famous red lights are in fact a combination of red and ultraviolet fluorescent tubes. The colour combination produces the ultimate artificial image. Form, skin tone and underwear are highlighted, facial detail and background surroundings are obscured. Rarely is light used to such precise effect.

Signs · City planning is based on politics and safety; more accurately, the politics of safety. The politics of safety produces a layering of signs, both vertically (signposts) and horizontally (painted graphics). At major junctions where pavements, cycle tracks, tram tracks and roads converge, the complexity is such that the individual signs become meaningless. The signs act as one collective sign, warning of complexity and danger ahead without giving any specific instructions.

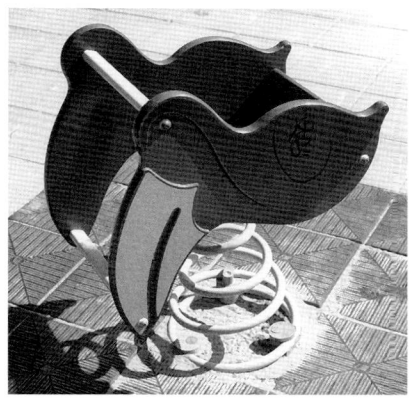

Springy toys · In every children's play area, small wooden animals are attached to metal springs which sprout from the ground. Children sit on the animals and rock to and fro. Children's play areas are everywhere. Amsterdam must have thousands of springs embedded in its surface.

Stairs · There are no grand staircases in Amsterdam. Amsterdam staircases are always steep. Houses have hoisting beams on their façades to enable furniture to be moved in and out (see above). Some open stairs are illuminated with intense blue light. On long, straight streets the effect of a large number of such stairs is visually arresting. The lights are blue in order to prevent junkies from 'shooting up' on the stairs. It is impossible to see veins under a blue light.

Taxi trap · A professor at the technical university of Delft has developed a special system to prevent taxis

driving too fast along tram lanes in the proximity of a tram stop. The road surface dips down on either side of the tram track. However, as the wheel spacing of taxis is the same as that of trams, taxi drivers regard it as a sort of game to see how fast they can 'fly' over the rails.

Telephone boxes · All telephone boxes belong to a single company, the PTT. They are all the same; bright green frame, large glass panels, clean and in working order.

Tram and bus stops · Always illuminated, always clean, each stop provides a map of the public transport system. Maintained by 'Publex', the system works perfectly, with the exception of one detail. The black circle with an arrow indicating your current location is often missing from the map. Without it, navigation to your desired destination is impossible, so that the entire stop is rendered useless.

Tram bells · Bells ring every time a tram pulls away from a stop. The constant ringing of tram bells is both comforting and very nostalgic. Only when something dares to block the tram's path does the bell change its tone; a continuous, shrill, urgent and impatient ring.

Wheel clamps · In the summer (maximum tourists) and in the inner city (maximum density), the bright yellow wheel clamp creates a sort of corporate identity for entire streets of illegally parked cars.

How to reach paradise · Details in urban space are like the smell of a dish. It can be fragrance, perfume and odour. It gives rise to expectations, promising pleasure or warning of poison. In architecture – of any kind – details present the intentions of the designer and signify how we are to understand and use the space as a whole.

Michelangelo knew how to design a flight of steps so that they meet a piazza in accordance with the human body. Tadao Ando chooses wall materials so as to let the light play with the texture.

And the right plants in a strictly designed garden help us to reach paradise.

THE CONSTRUCTIONAL DETAIL

HARRY EVERS

Let us define detail as 'a small part, a particular', but note that the structural engineer must, of necessity, concentrate on the constructional detail: that part of the construction which connects or accentuates elements. What for others is a subordinate part of a building is sometimes a main element for the structural engineer.

Looking at the city at the level of the detail, one wonders what special details are to be found in the cityscape, how visible and palpable are they, and what ideas do they embody? Has the detail been determined by architectural considerations, by the logic of the construction, or is it, as it were, undesigned?

Regrettably, anyone who looks at the cityscape will observe that the detail is seldom given adequate attention. This is the case in Amsterdam and in the country as a whole. Amsterdam is a city which (partly because it was never the seat of the Dutch court with its ambience conducive to culture) has always set a higher value on commerce than on crafts. For centuries, earning money

Ellermeijer
[Dome
Architecten,
1989]

has been more important than culture, and the Dutch mentality embodied in the saying, 'act normally, that's crazy enough', has always prevailed. Consequently, architecture in Amsterdam is simpler than in the capital cities of neighbouring countries, and there has never been much room for exuberance. Architecture here invariably seems to have to look as if it represents 'value for money'.

Amsterdam-Zuidoost · On closer consideration of the details in the city, there are a few structures which catch the eye. Let us look first at a building in Amsterdam-Zuidoost, the so-called 'high-tech' construction, realized for car company Ellermeijer (design: Dome Architecten, 1989).

The building is characterized by large quantities of exuberant steel and the double tension-members are also impressive. However, as a structural engineer, one immediately spots an inconsistency. The diagonal rods

A-*point*
[René Jacobs,
1993]

have been secured between triangular bogies, but the
vertical rods have not. The resultant differences in
length and tensile force are compensated for by turnbuckles, which are conspicuous partly because of the
strong colour contrast. The baseplate detail with its
large, deep splits (which are impossible to maintain) is
highly susceptible to corrosion. The oversize trusses are
stabilized and prevented from toppling over by means
of a veritable network of 16-millimetre-thin rods (in
conjunction with so-called 'hinged' connections with
two bolts).

Thus, in the top view of this connection, all that
seems to be lacking are the indications (by means of
black arrows, for example) of the paths of lines of force
in the various details. Better and more balanced detailing could have helped the building to do justice to the
prominent site. A missed opportunity indeed.

Not far from this building is a structure with one
special detail. This is the building 'A-point' (architect:

René Jacobs, 1993) which, with the exception of the entrance, is rather dull and uninteresting, but which does at least have a clear constructional concept. The building's canteen rests on four double columns which are not situated at the angular points, but rather in the middle of the sides. The roof and the floors are suspended from four open triangular structures and the volume is encased in a glass façade.

A striking feature of this structure is the self-evident way in which the details relate to each other. Perhaps because the three-dimensional qualities of the details were first evaluated by computer (as a result of which the interrelated proportions could be coordinated), and because each plate and hanger has a function, a self-reinforcing effect is produced. Each detail seems to have sprung naturally from another. As a result, the entire construction, including the visible interplay of forces, is perceived as logical, even by non-specialists, who are feeling safe under it.

Telephone tower · Closer to the city centre, in Buitenveldert, stands the 106-metre-high DC2 telephone tower. In 1987, two levels (to a design by Cepezed) were added to the existing concrete telephone tower. The problem was that, because of the transmitters, the maximum angular displacement in wind could not exceed 0.5 degrees, while the existing concrete mast could not sustain more than 100 tons.

These requirements have resulted in a simple, rational solution. The floors have been realized as saucer-shaped wings, that is, as plate constructions which function as a disc and have little wind catch. Stability is achieved because the columns intersect diagonally.

DC2
*telephone
tower*
[Cepezed,
1987]

Partly because there are very few connecting points on the existing structure and the connections are simple hinged connections, construction was easy and it was completed in a single day.

Although all the details are at a height of between 80 and 106 metres, and are therefore not easy to see, the designers have given considerable thought to how the various connections would be perceived, and in particular to whether these connections should be countersunk and out of sight, or be clearly visible. Eventually, it was decided that the saucers should be continued and the joints clearly visible. This was the best solution technically, and from the point of view of production and maintenance (corrosion). The clarity of the structure also means that it is pleasing architecturally.

Canopies · On the edge of the city centre, near the start of Ferdinand Bolstraat, in 1995 a new complex of shops and dwellings was built to a design by De Jong

Heineken-terrein
[De Jong Hoogveld De Kat, 1995]

Stadhouders-kade
[Hans van Heeswijk, 1991]

➤

Hoogveld De Kat. It is a large complex with one striking feature: the canopy near one of the side entrances. It seems that all the mistakes that can be made in designing have been made in this structure – unless they are intentional.

The four double-acting turnbuckles, which in fact could have been omitted, have been tightened to the same extent so that they are in the same position (as if the tension in the tie-rod is irrelevant). The cantilevered profile is a tapered, bisected beam which has been reinforced on the underside with a narrow strip, perhaps in order to prevent the vertical leg from buckling, although it is doubtful whether this was necessary because the many partitions with their fork-restrained ends also prevent buckling. Water and dirt accumulate in the U-profiles attached to the front. In order to give an appearance of transparency, a fluorescent tube has been incorporated in the enormous concrete socle. The longer one looks at the construction, the more one is

astonished that so many rules could be violated on such a small surface area (the canopy measures only two by three metres).

Fortunately, around the corner, on Stadhouders-kade, is a striking and successful structure: an office building, built in 1991 to a design by Hans van Hees-wijk. This building differs from the adjacent structures in all respects and yet it relates well to the site. The only possible explanation for this lies in the honesty and purity of the lines of the building and of its details. Each element here has a function and this clarity is a delight to the eye.

Here, for example, is a canopy which construction-ally clearly projects from within, but on the outside is architecturally so separate from the building that one expects to see columns or suspension cables. This is in conjunction with a bridging beam which also serves as a gutter. The most striking feature is the lift construc-tion. Set back slightly in relation to the frontage of the main building and somewhat enclosed, one large glass surface has been created which (unlike most glass struc-tures) has a tranquil presence.

The attachments of the colossal glass plates are themselves worth studying. Wind forces are transmit-ted inconspicuously via the slender supporting struc-ture behind to the floors. In order to ensure that the glass plates can expand freely, each plate is suspended from four stainless-steel strips which can revolve on the underside.

Why does this building delight the eye? Because of its apparent simplicity, a self-evident design without

Housing and office, Kerkstraat [Sjoerd Soeters, 1996/1989]

superfluous frills, as regards both the supporting structure and the smallest details.

Old Dutch · Finally, something quite different. Not
far from the last building (in Kerkstraat) there is art.
Next to an old Dutch restaurant, Sjoerd Soeters has
given an existing chapel a new façade and built a new
complex up against it. The first volume, Soeters' architectural office, flirts with the idea of high-tech. The
façade is composed of corrugated aluminium plates
which accentuate the diagonals of the façade surface.
Bays immediately behind divide the façade into com-
prehensible parts – a good example of careful detailing.
   The new building, with office spaces on the ground
floor and apartments above, looks like three individual
houses incorporated in a single, completely symmet-
rical whole. Here, every detail is an ornament and the
interrelationships are so logical that one can look at
these three houses as if they were a large painting in

brick. This impression is reinforced by the contrast with the adjacent aluminium façade.

The entire complex in Kerkstraat shows that detailing is not so much a question of harmony or contrast. Nor is it about how contemporary or historical a detail should be. It can all exist side by side if the detailing is carefully and lovingly executed. This holds true for the large, well-known buildings (which I have not discussed here) and for the buildings just around the corner.

Detailing in Amsterdam: that is the gigantic Amsterdam Arena, the new Ajax stadium, but also the streamlined, ingeniously designed carrier bicycle. What is important is that every element and every detail has a function. A city can be great in small things too.

Movement · The clinker cladding forms a smooth surface which is enlivened by reflections. Moreover, the game of the windows on the side sets the façade in motion. As a result, on the south side, in the direction of the pier, the danger of a static frontality is averted.

(Statement accompanying the design for the housing [1995] in the Eastern Docklands, Amsterdam)

DETAILS IN PUBLIC SPACE

GUUSJE TER HORST

A detail is a small part of a whole. If we conceive the public space as a whole and the street furniture as a small component, then the street furniture is a detail. And wandering around the centre of Amsterdam, the first thing that strikes us is the enormous diversity of this type of detail: bicycle racks, litter bins, drinking fountains, ticket-machines, electricity boxes, bottle banks and paper igloos, traffic signs, benches, lamp-posts, post-boxes, advertising signs, tram and bus shelters, flower boxes, advertising columns, bollards, urinals, transformer kiosks, hydrants, telephone boxes – you name it.

The much admired street furniture of the first half of the twentieth century, designed by the architects of the Amsterdam School, has virtually disappeared from the city. Notable survivals from the past are the Amsterdammertjes and the so-called 'krul' (curl), a public urinal, which comes in a single as well as in a double version.

Urinating · Urinating in public has always been a problem in Amsterdam. There was a ban on urinating in public as early as the sixteenth century, and since the nineteenth century a by-law has restricted this act. At the beginning of this century the need for public conveniences was recognized, but at the same time there was a fear that the urinal might function as a meeting place for homosexuals: 'The design and positioning of the urinal had to be such that a police officer would be able to see at a glance how many men were inside the urinal. This had consequences for the design. It had to have a certain "openness", without being too open. The problem was solved by leaving the lower part of the urinal open so that legs would be visible and by perforating the iron walls of the curl' (Kasper van Ommen in: *Straatmeubilair Amsterdamse School 1911-1940*, Amsterdam, 1992).

For all that, when in the eighties the city council decided to remove the curls, homosexual interest

groups were up in arms: the curls were, after all, important national (and international) meeting places for gays. That they still have this function today is perhaps due to the tolerance praised by the poet Nico Scheepmaker in his poem 'Zeven eeuwen Amsterdam' (Seven centuries of Amsterdam):

The nicest thing about the city must be that
there still exists a bit of tolerance, as they say.
My dearest wish would be to go on holiday
to Amsterdam as one who's never been there yet.

The Amsterdammertje first came into use about two hundred years ago. Today, there are almost 70,000 bollards in the city centre as an anti-parking device, with the result that motorists are inclined to think that parking is allowed wherever there are no bollards. In order to reduce the number of Amsterdammertjes, it has been decided that they should be placed only where they are really necessary; for example, in areas where there are no suitable alternatives and where towing away cars would be an endless task.

Policy · In this respect Amsterdam's policy regarding the bollard is exemplary, because stringent standards need to be established for the design, siting and maintenance of all the city's street furniture. There is ample evidence of this need in the city centre: for instance, the litter bins or the electricity boxes which seem to have been parachuted at random, instead of being carefully positioned (the worst example is the electricity box placed between two benches, so that people sitting opposite each other cannot see each other), the same

electricity boxes which suddenly are no longer dark green, but grey; the bottle banks and paper igloos which were originally intended to be temporary, but which have long been an affront to the city; the fluorescent green telephone boxes which catch the eye, but which are out of keeping with the decor of the city centre; and all the objects which because of their lack of paint are a blot on the cityscape.

It has to be said that durability often takes precedence over aesthetic considerations in the design of street furniture, that objects are sited without respect for the surrounding area, and that, due to lack of funds, maintenance leaves much to be desired.

A requirement street furniture ought to meet is that it is appropriate to the historic city centre. Furthermore, although standardization of street furniture is necessary, there ought to be room for exceptions. Recently, Amsterdam city council has acted in accordance with this principle in two recent projects: the

Bench,
Damrak
[Schabracq
& Postma,
1992]

design for the street furniture of the unique Nieuw-markt square and the important axis Damrak-Rokin, for which the artists Alexander Schabracq and Tom Postma were engaged as designers.

Both cases have shown that exceptions inevitably provoke irritation, but can also evoke unexpected positive reactions. The Amsterdam writer Frans Pointl wrote (in: *Het centrum van de wereld*, Amsterdam, 1992): 'There is the new street furniture which I have only seen from the tram. The tax revenues have been put to good use for once. I go and sit down. The bench is like a work of art that belongs in a museum. To the left and right a sculpture, in between the armrest. The colour is greenish blue, but I'm slightly colour blind. If you are a tourist and are photographed on this bench, you take an original work of art home with you.'

Art in public space · Art objects in public space can also be regarded as details. They do not always have a

utility value, like street furniture, but are an embellishment of the public space of Amsterdam. Less visible than street furniture, sometimes even concealed and perceived only by the passer-by with an eye for detail, dozens of works of art are scattered over the city. Perhaps the fact that they are partially hidden increases their appeal, as in the case of the monument to the astronomer Arago in Paris (the 135 circular copper plaques, designed by the Dutch artist Jan Dibbets, in the paving of streets, parks and squares); or, to take an example closer to home, the poetry route in Leeuwarden, in which poems on the paving stones lead you through the city.

In Amsterdam, there are quite a few statues of writers. Some people regard these at best as 'details which you hardly notice', others take pleasure in being able to stand face to face with Dutch literary figures of the past, such as Bredero, Multatuli and Herman Heijermans. The statue of the writer and schoolteacher

Theo Thijssen and his hero Kees de Jongen (Kees the Boy), on a busy spot in the city (filled-in Lindengracht), inspired the poet Martin Veltman to sigh:

I greet the old man Thijssen and the boy,
and in the classroom see myself again.
Master who led the singing, where and when
have the cantatas gone of love and joy?
– So the canal without the water it had then.

Near Leidseplein, you are surprised to see some thirty lizards and other reptiles, by the artist Hans van Houwelingen. Here, too, is the city's most concealed work of art: the nameless statue of a man sawing through the branch on which he is standing. Have a drink in one of the many pavement cafés in the area and reflect on what the highly popular writer Simon Carmiggelt, for many years the most important chronicler of Amsterdam (café) life, once said:

I like to sit in an old pub in Amsterdam,
silently musing among friends – I love it dearly.
If only closing time, for me and most of them,
were not always too late, and yet always too early.

Carmiggelt died not so long ago, and there is a bronze statue of him in a small park within walking distance of Leidseplein.

Gardens · The municipal government had a hand in producing most of the objects in public space discussed

Self-help project: Schone Weespad

above. Increasingly, however (and this is an encouraging trend), local residents and entrepreneurs are taking responsibility for the quality of their environment. In many places in the city this has resulted in so-called 'self-help projects', whereby, in consultation with the city council, residents design, create and maintain gardens and play areas.

In addition, the council considers the cooperation of home-owners to be vital to the success of the newly launched project 'Graffiti Fini', which is aimed at cleaning the city centre and keeping it clean. Our sense of well-being in the city is not only influenced by architectural details; flyposting, graffiti and, last but not least, dog excrement also have an effect on the quality of our environment. The tightening-up and enforcement of regulations with regard to such matters are of vital importance.

One could say: it is impossible to please everyone, even at the level of details. The youngest residents are deprived of an ideal hole for their game of marbles when a footpath is perfectly paved, and there is always someone who is annoyed because the long-awaited litter bin has been placed right in front of his or her front door. It is the responsibility of the city council to preserve the (unstable) equilibrium.

And this is what the council is aiming to do with the city centre project whose slogan is: 'Cleaner, more beautiful and emptier'. 'More beautiful' is particularly difficult. Perhaps the city needs some sort of urban design control similar to that which governs the building process. There will always be debate of course, which is a good thing. What one person finds beautiful may not be so to someone else, even, or perhaps especially, when it comes to details.

Bar code · The most important detail in Amsterdam is the window frame. It is the master joiner's drawing in wide and narrow white lines which, in contrast with the dark masonry, determines the Breitnerian image of the city centre. The thinness of the façade skin with its shallow reveal in conjunction with the here wider, there deeper wood of the window frame, and the different dimensions of the windows set within, creates an image of alternating vertical white and black lines along the street façade. Cycling along the canal, I see Amsterdam as constantly varying strips of bar code.

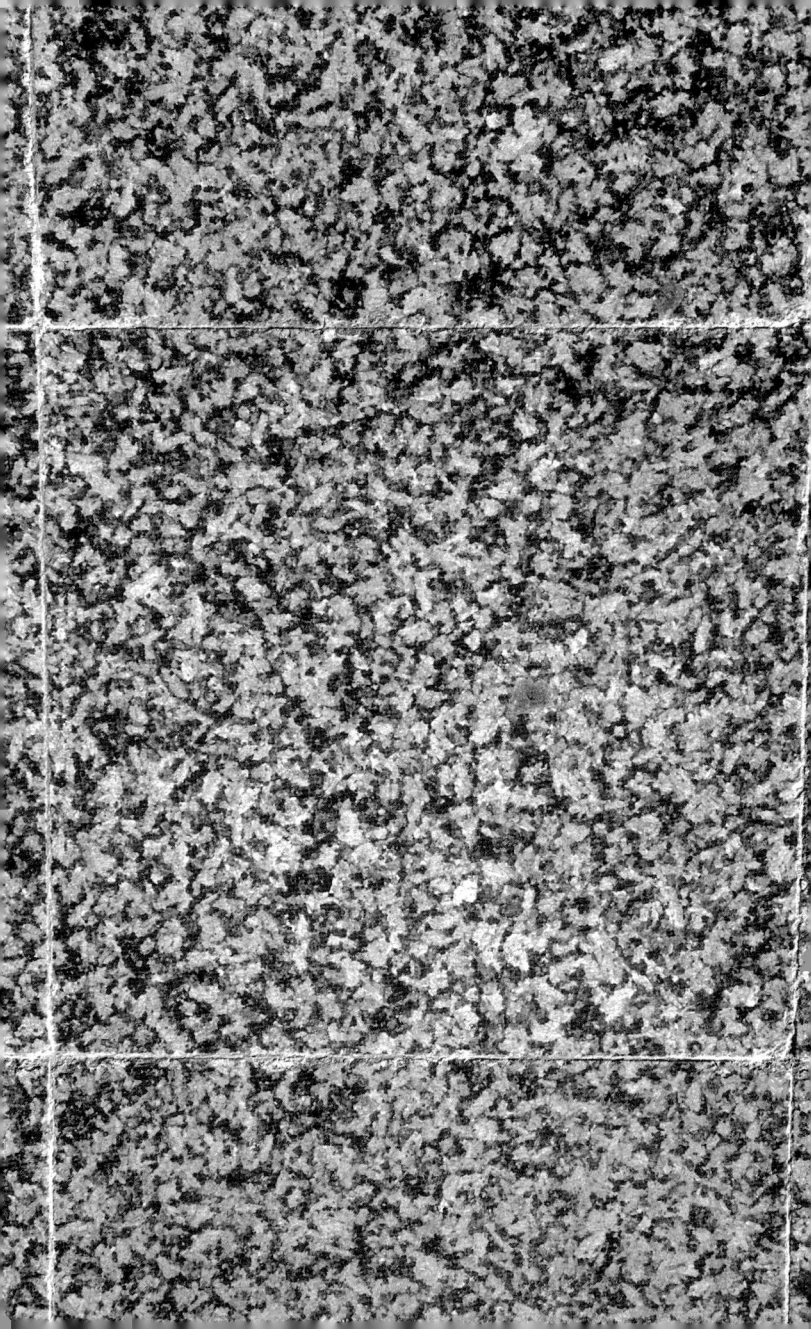

THE COSMOPOLITAN DETAIL

STAN ALLEN

Jane Jacobs, well known to architectural readers as the author of *The Death and Life of Great American Cities* (London, 1974), has written a fascinating book on morality, commerce and politics. Presented in narrative form, her new book is entitled *Systems of Survival: A Dialogue on the Moral Foundations of Commerce and Politics* (New York, 1994).

The title itself hints at the direction the text will take. Jacobs is not interested in passing judgement or calling for radical change. Rather, recognizing the existence of many strategies to survive and prosper in today's complex world, she has been motivated to look at the interplay between moral codes and the everyday conduct of business and government. No anti-foundationalist, Jacobs nonetheless steers clear of an essentialist appeal to universal structures of morality by proposing not one, but two moral codes.

These codes, which Jacobs calls 'syndromes', from the Greek 'things that run together', emerge from the classification of a series of precepts that govern the behaviour of distinct occupational groups within societies. The first she calls the 'Commercial Moral Syndrome', and it is characterized by values of free exchange and open association. Hence, precepts such as 'Come to voluntary agreements' or 'Collaborate easily with strangers and aliens' appear here.

This first syndrome is fundamentally optimistic, and embraces enterprise and inventiveness. Although conventional values such as honesty and efficiency follow, the value of dissent is also recognized as necessary in order to maintain open exchange. Going beyond cultural or national values, Jacobs asserts that 'These precepts rule wherever commercial life is viable, East or West. They apply to Islamic innkeepers, Buddhist batik makers, Hindu brass craftsmen, Shinto brake manufacturers, just as they do to Christian, Jewish or atheist auto mechanics or potters [...].'

Opposed to the commercial syndrome is the 'Guardian Moral Syndrome'. Here Jacobs appears to follow Thorstein Veblen in *The Theory of the Leisure Class* (London, 1970), who saw the origins of the leisure class in the ancient castes of warriors and priests – guardian figures who were exempt from the productive life of the community and were charged instead with the visible exemplification of moral codes through ritual and conspicuous consumption.

Ritual behaviour · Indeed, there is a strong component of ritual behaviour underlying the precepts Jacobs identifies with the guardian syndrome: 'Respect hierarchy', 'Be disciplined' and 'Adhere to tradition'. These are the precepts that guide the behaviour of governments and their bureaucracies, as well as the armed forces and the police. They apply to religious hierarchies and to the traditional ruling classes (aristocracies and landed gentry). Honour, rather than prosperity or comfort, is an ultimate guardian value. Where the commercial syndrome eschews the use of force and emphasizes negotiation, the guardian syndrome is suspicious of trading, which so often requires compromise.

The display of strength and the use of force are characteristic of this second syndrome: 'taking' as opposed to 'trading'. While the commercial syndrome recognizes the need to be flexible and to 'dissent for the sake of the task', the guardian syndrome allows for a certain moral flexibility with regard to means and ends: 'Deceive for the sake of the task' suggests that, under certain conditions, strict honesty may be compromised for the sake of larger principles. Government-sponsored deceptions such as wartime secrecy, spying or propaganda come to mind here. Finally, the ostentatious use of leisure time and the dispensation of largesse belong to the guardian syndrome and recall Veblen's ideas of conspicuous consumption.

Jacobs is scrupulously fair-minded, and her argument is not so much in favour of one syndrome over another, as for maintenance of the distinction. She intends the book to serve as a caution against the confusion that results from mixing the syndromes. It is, however, difficult not to detect a faint bias on Jacob's part in favour of the commercial moral syndrome over the guardian one. In her discussion of science, for example, she quotes T.H. Huxley to the effect that 'Science and her methods gave me a resting place independent of tradition and authority'. The values of science – independent investigation, openness to the results of experimental inquiry, which may or may not be in agreement with received doctrine – correspond closely with commercial values. 'Science is open to novelty. It is inventive. It demands initiative and enterprise.' More importantly, science has always cultivated open exchange and collaboration with strangers. Science is linked to a cultural prospect that is cosmopolitan and urban.

Hybrid · What, does all of this have to do with architecture in general and Amsterdam in particular?

Interestingly enough, Jacobs does not mention architecture, although in a brief discussion she suggests that the arts are *sui generis* defying categorization. I would suggest that architecture is something of a hybrid. Its origins in ritual link it to guardian culture. Architecture's first patrons were priests and warrior chiefs. But since the Renaissance, we can detect a shift away from the patronage of the church and the court.

The emergence of a powerful merchant class and a sophisticated urban culture marks a shift away from architecture as an embodiment of guardian values to an engagement with the complex and contradictory culture of commerce. Even today, architects are licensed and regulated by the state to perform guardian functions, yet they operate for the most part within a commercial culture. Some of the confusion in the architectural profession today is probably traceable to this contradiction. Architects are trained to think of themselves as guardians, yet the reality of the practice of architecture today is almost entirely subject to the rule of the market-place.

To return to the culture of cities, we could use this distinction to elaborate Jacobs' earlier thinking. The urban values that Jacobs writes so favourably about in *The Death and Life of Great American Cities* and *The Economy of Cities* (Harmondsworth, 1972) – diversity, small scale, local control, mixed uses, incremental change and bottom-up government – belong almost exclusively to the commercial syndrome. To put her work in context, it could be read as an extended polemic against a professional culture of urbanism that was, in the late 1950s, overly dominated by guardian values: regulation, zoning, hierarchy and the separation of functions, slum clearance and heroic rebuilding. The city of the Athens Charter was a city of guardian values, and capitals such as Brasilia or Chandigarh embodied these values in concrete form.

Contrast this with the definition of *cosmopolitan* advanced in the *Systems of Survival*: 'The principal places in which strangers do business together are big cities. The cosmopolitanism of those cities is no accident [...]. To make mundane, everyday deals with strangers and aliens demands tolerance for people outside one's own background and personal preferences [...]. Cosmopolitanism spills over into other fields, such as the arts, but its roots are commercial.'

Now Amsterdam, more than any other city in Europe, embodies these cosmopolitan values. It is a city deeply marked by its mercantile culture and is representative of many of the precepts identified by Jacobs as belonging to the commercial moral syndrome. Thrift, industry, honesty and initiative are highly valued within Amsterdam's urban culture and, I would suggest, are visible in the physical fabric of the city itself. It is a city

refreshingly open to strangers and to ideas and culture from outside. Innovation and enterprise do not appear to contradict traditional values and a respect for history. In fact, it might be said that in Amsterdam, in as much as its deepest traditions are mercantile, modern values of efficiency, change and innovation do not openly conflict with that tradition.

Transparency · As a visitor, I was struck by the open character of the small houses that make up so much of the fabric of historic Amsterdam. They seem to anticipate Modern Movement ideas of transparency, lightness and the direct expression of structure. For someone used to the paranoia of New York, or to the shuttered cities of Southern Europe, it is astonishing to walk on the streets in the evening and look in on a family seated at dinner or a businessman working late; all exposed to the life of the street without intervening shades or curtains. (This of course reaches something of an extreme

in the redlight district, which is, after all, yet another expression of an open-minded commercial culture.) Moreover, looking into a medieval house and discovering a modern interior presents no great sense of discontinuity. Old and new coexist comfortably.

I later discovered that this openness was a direct result of building types developed for the merchant class, the 'houten onderpui' (wooden shop front), a type of construction that has the effect of making the house appear to float off the ground. As Karl Kiem wrote in 'Windows All Over': 'The masonry wall surfaces above were opened up to the extent that surface dominates over mass' (*Daidalos*, 33, September 1989). Business was conducted on the ground floor and on the street, blurring the distinction between public and private space.

In the numerous examples of Modern Movement buildings in Amsterdam, this same degree of openness is preserved and even intensified. Duiker's Openluchtschool on Cliostraat represents a high point in the culture of literal transparency. Enclosing membranes are reduced to a delicate minimum. In Dutch modernist architecture, window frames – which are themselves lightweight and of minimum profile – are typically brought forward, rather than recessed, which further emphasizes the lightness of the structure. And more recently, a kind of contemporary Dutch vernacular has emerged (not limited to Amsterdam), visible in the work of Koolhaas and younger architects, and consisting of translucent sheathing, screens of perforated metal and corrugated metal skin.

But the Modern Movement brings something else, more ideological, to the culture of openness. Functional transparency as well as literal transparency is evident in the Cineac Cinema (unfortunately, it was in a neglected state when I saw it recently). Here, in a building type closely linked with cosmopolitan culture, the architecture registers the complexity of the internal functions in both volume and detail. The extension of the building upwards in the open scaffold of the billboard has the effect of rendering the entire structure provisional. Structure and mass are decomposed into sign, surface and framework. That this results in a building entirely at home in its small-scale pedestrian street is all the more remarkable, but, to my view, is typical of the city.

Rietveld · The quality of openness is expressed differently in the case of the Netherlands' most famous modernist. What is unique about Rietveld's detailing is

Housing Binnen Wieringerstraat [Claus & Kaan, 1995]

a sense that, with only a minimal knowledge of architecture, the ordinary visitor might understand exactly how the building has been put together. Standard sections, minimal manipulation of materials, exposed fasteners. Everything laid out, as if in evidence. There is no mystery to the construction, no hermetic guardian secrets.

If we understand architecture, as I believe we must, not as high culture, aloof from everyday reality and the intricacies of exchange, but as a practice intimately linked with the economic life of a city and its citizens, it is hard not to see Amsterdam's architecture as a reflection of its mercantile culture. This is what distinguishes Amsterdam from other European cities, and can be identified as consistent throughout historical and stylistic variation.

The dedicated reader of academic literature will no doubt recognize two cardinal sins in this short text. First, a too easy acceptance of a binary schema, and second, sweeping generalization along national or ethnic lines. The oppositional schema proposed by Jane Jacobs is no doubt open to criticism on many grounds. My own sense is that it pays insufficient attention to the grey areas, to all of those paradoxical, unclassifiable mixtures that to me always seem more interesting than unadulterated quantities. Nor do I doubt that the characteristic Dutch 'openness' is much more complex and subtle than I have described. My starting-point has been the architecture. If the case has been overstated, it is in an effort to get at what seemed to me to be peculiar to this architecture and to this place.

Gerrit Rietveld Academie [G.Th. Rietveld, 1967]

AD · It is only possible to talk about architectural detail (AD) as if its function is to produce an effect, when it is assumed that the detail indeed arises out of this background. I am of the opinion, however, that today the AD is first and foremost determined by functionality or producibility in the assemblage of materials. Now that the elaborateness of the detail – because of the available budgets – is increasingly being reduced to a minimum, it appears that the reproduction of old images, such as the game of joints and dimensions in the façades of the Amsterdam School, or the play of light and shadow in Gothic and Baroque vaulted constructions, are things of the past. I am of the opinion that current references to these old methods are apt to look ridiculous or excessively sentimental.

Today, the architect is reduced to taking the viewer with him in the (logical) process of assembling products – scant consolation. The object of the architect might then be to show the intentions. The AD then shows the degree of closed quality, openness and clarity, rhythm, smoothness or roughness of the material. With regard to the interior, these considerations can still be worked out intelligibly. With regard to the exterior, there is limited scope; the detail is determined *en sec* and debate about material finish is fuelled by the hysteria surrounding the inspectability and lifetime of buildings, rather than by 'sensitive' arguments based on tradition.

Recent publications highlight the fiasco all too well: an unusual brick pattern or jointing format is already regarded as a rarity and acclaimed as unique. What is beyond dispute, however, is that the AD has significantly contributed to the image of beautiful cities: our environment is becoming impoverished indeed!

ODE TO MY AMSTERDAM
BERNT LUGER

They say that couples who grow old together do not notice changes in each other's appearance, but this does not hold true for cities in which one has lived all one's life. One does not need old photographs of the city one has become attached to in order to notice changes, chiefly because changes in the city are seldom improvements, but almost always brazen interventions which one never gets used to. In the city, there is the pain of the loss and one 'sees' that which has disappeared with the eye of memory. A few examples.

Decay · Not so long ago, I read that the old monumental bridge linking Vondelpark with what was to have been a well-to-do residential area to the south of the park had fallen into disrepair. I cycle practically every week over this bridge and have never noticed anything other than the familiar image of pointless grandeur and loss. The cracks in the weathered stone have been there ever since I was a child and used to walk

Vondelpark

across the bridge to go skating near the children's farm in the park (now a noisy and profitable fun-fair). May this bridge be preserved in its dilapidated state – with all the wrinkles and crow's-feet which have always, or so it seems, graced its face – for my children and grand-children.

Of course, common sense tells me that I am deceiving myself. For we ourselves, at the chance moment of our conscious perception, determine the norm on that random reference date. Half a century ago the bridge, for whoever fixed it in their memory, was a different bridge, and in another fifty years' time it will be different from the bridge it is today. Thus, my children and grandchildren will have their own reference dates on which their norms are determined.

Often, such a moment of conscious perception and filing away in one's memory is linked to casual associations: here lived a schoolfriend, in that square I saw my first real traffic accident, in that street I once saw the fire brigade swing into action. A ladder had been placed high up against the façade of the building and I saw smoke coming out of the attic window. An architectural detail such as the imitation Renaissance façade is filed away in my memory and I like to make a detour in order to see that façade again. The present residents of the house suspect nothing, I think.

Something similar is true of measurements and proportions. Almost always, the house and the street in which we grew up seem smaller than we remember when we visit them years later. That should teach us that measurements are relative. Children's eyes measure differently, adults are giants and old people. The distortion is the same as that produced by spectacles: anyone who puts on spectacles for the first time realizes how relative perception is.

Beauty · Our aesthetic sense has a reference date too, its relative norm which is often regarded as absolute. I remember as a child walking through the city hand in hand with my father. We passed the Rijksmuseum (P.J.H. Cuypers, 1885), which to me was neither beautiful nor ugly, but extremely impressive. My father pointed with annoyance to the tourists taking photographs of the building.

'Those idiots can't even see how ugly it is!'
'Why is it ugly, papa?'
'Because it is the epitome of bastardization. Neo-Gothic and bastardized too, with squat towers.'

The above took place in the days when a continuous ring of imposing houses graced Weteringschans; the

Rijksmuseum
[P.J.H.
Cuypers,
1885]

*Office
buildings,
Wetering-
schans*
[F.J. van
Gool, 1979]

row of bourgeois monuments which the Dutch painter Carel Willink has so often immortalized from his studio window. Nowadays opposite the Rijksmuseum are two office bunkers which the Amsterdammers were quick to christen the 'salt-cellar and pepper-pot'. With their embrasures, they look as if they could withstand every attack, except perhaps – unfortunately – that of decay. I shall never get used to these functional monstrosities. Nor shall I ever get used to demolition.

A few years ago, I bought a tray in a jumble sale on which is painted (behind glass) a picture of the Willebrordus church (designed by Cuypers) on the river Amstel. When it was built (1899), it was situated on the outskirts of the city. I cannot say whether the church was beautiful or ugly, but I do lament the fact that it has been demolished and I always miss it when I cross the Amstel and see on the site where the church once stood a modern sort of warehouse for old-age pensioners.

Looking at my tray, I notice something curious, something unreal. This rather crude picture (painting behind glass is a difficult art) shows the church with towers which do not correspond with reality as regards their length and number. A comparison with old photographs of the building confirms my suspicions. My tray shows the church as Cuypers originally intended it to look.

It appears that Cuypers had envisaged a complete cathedral complex, with even a large and monumental cemetery next to the church. It was to have been Cuypers' crowning architectural achievement. However, what was finally built was 'bastardized' neo-Gothic, just as crippled as the Rijksmuseum and Centraal Station (1889), because intrusive Catholic manifestations were not welcome in this predominantly Protestant city. My tray is, as it were, a correction of history, but pointless now that the building has been demolished.

Ornaments · In the light of the above, the concept of 'architectural details' is also put into perspective and subjected to my personal perception. In the eyes of a child, they are always ornaments, like those by the sculptor Hildo Krop which can be seen on bridges and street corners throughout Amsterdam-Zuid.

The way in which I used to look at these ornaments as a child was moreover strongly influenced by the stories my father used to tell. My father was a painter and a friend of Krop's. When they were both poor artists starting out on their careers, they used to do each other good turns. For example, Krop once made a wooden bookcase for my father, the top corners of which were ornamented with the stylized owls characteristic of Krop's work. In exchange, my father painted decorative pictures around the stove-pipe below Hildo Krop's chimney-pieces.

Unlike Krop's bridges and façade details, these details could only be viewed indoors, but they do have something in common: the chimney-pieces have disappeared behind modern gas fires, or have been painted over by new residents, and Krop's ornaments on houses and bridges have been spoiled by overpainting and air pollution. Everywhere, pockmarked horses and children stare at us with sightless eyes. The head of Rubens (in Rubensstraat) is now an amorphous plum pudding, and only the sculpted letters below the head proclaim the name of this lumpy dish.

Rubens
[Hildo Krop,
1928]

Attention to ornament also leads to other experiences. In 1995, attention was focused on the bridges built by the Amsterdam School architect Piet Kramer in Amsterdam-Zuid. This was by means of small exhibitions of photographs on the parapets of the bridges. Partly in order to see Krop's ornaments, I visited a few of these exhibitions, particularly those near the gateway below the school the Amsterdams Lyceum in Valeriusplein.

One photograph showed the bridge shortly after its completion, with in the background the recently completed school building. As a former pupil of the school, I noticed a detail which I hesitate to call architectural: two sunblinds on the south façade which, as an insider, I knew were situated above the rooms of the teachers and the headmaster. I turned round and saw sunblinds above all the classrooms. They are probably more of sociological than architectural significance, as are the barred windows on the ground floor; one a sign of

◄
Amsterdams Lyceum, south façade [H.A.J. & J. Baanders, 1920]

House Beethoven-straat/ Apollolaan [A. Wester-man, 1954]

humanization, the other a sign of urban criminality. It reminds me that as a child I witnessed the bombardment of the buildings of the German Sicherheitsdienst on what was then called Euterpestraat (now Gerrit van der Veenstraat). Afterwards, we used to play in the ruins of the buildings and houses which, through lack of funds, were not restored or replaced until long after the war. I can still point out the differences between old and new, slight though they are. Sometimes, the new buildings give themselves away; for instance, because of the style of restoration of the styleless fifties (see the two houses on the corner of Beethovenstraat and Apollolaan).

Vanished cityscapes · Most of my personal architectural details were part of cityscapes now vanished, and which I see in my mind's eye whenever I look at the ugly buildings that have replaced them: the churches which were demolished to make way for the Marriott Hotel

and the University Library, the dilapidated Muziek-
lyceum (which has been set fire to several times) and the
riding school opposite which were replaced by the far
too tall Hilton Hotel.

Do trees form part of the city's architecture?
Originally, they were intended to provide a bit of nature
in the wide, quiet streets, but the proliferating lay-
bys are encroaching on the trees' spaces and they are
exposed to harmful car exhaust fumes. Trees are of
course part of the city's 'street furniture', as were the
blue giro-boxes which have now disappeared from
the landscape. Until recently, I did not realize that these
had been designed in the style of the Amsterdam
School, as were the small municipal buildings which
once dotted the city, and which I used to think con-
tained dangerous electrical machinery. In reality, they
housed the council's cleaning equipment and, together
with the newspaper kiosks, most were demolished
before people could be alerted to this outrage.

When as a child I attended Duiker's Openluchtschool, I was unaware of the fact that I was learning to read and write in an architectural masterwork. I did though sometimes see tourists in the school playground, strangers with huge cameras around their necks who immortalized the school in their photographs. We took little notice of these visitors who saw what we did not see. Now I know better: they saw what we did not yet or no longer see.

We sat at the modern school desks and innocently sang the school song, which included the lines:

With your windows open,
to the side where the sunlight is.

We were aware thus that our school was different from other schools. In my memory, everything was glass set in steel window frames which were painted blue, and in the summer we had our lessons on the balconies. For health was synonymous with light and air and the name of the school was a programme: Open Air School for the Healthy Child. However, it was only when I stood looking at it next to a tourist with his camera that I saw that remarkable angular building for the first time.

Visiting Amsterdam · Someone once wrote that a major disadvantage of living in Amsterdam is that one never goes to Amsterdam. One ought to leave the city for a considerable length of time and then return. Leave Amsterdam in order to forget daily purposiveness and free oneself from all that is ordinary and everyday. Or, what also helps sometimes, see something in a special light or in an imaginary frame.

On a sunny late afternoon, turn the corner of Heren-gracht/Nieuwe Spiegelstraat and walk along the latter street. The eye is immediately drawn to the eastern tower of the Rijksmuseum in the distance, silhouetted against the light of the setting sun. Our aesthetic sense at that moment is undoubtedly conditioned by all those paintings and postcards of streets in the Jordaan look-ing towards the Westertoren. But that does not matter, because for everyone it is new just for a moment and belongs only to the viewer. In such frames, details are seen and verified as if through the eye of a camera.

Lacking touchability · *Buildings, to start with them, which are conceived without marked attention to* DETAIL *and consequently lack physical place-quality; specific locality and, let me emphasize this:* touchability, *are not only shamefully deficient – but, in my view, barely on the way towards completion – this, I'm afraid, goes for most of them. The truth is, that without real attention to such matters as these, space – architectural space, hence architecture itself – will simply not come about: not in buildings and* certainly not in cities, *which are now fast becoming manipulated wastelands. Not their inhabitants are at fault in the first place, but an entirely new brand of trend-receptive 'masterminds', who are currently misleading feeble-minded authorities. Indeed, for buildings, as wel as for cities where multitudes of people move around more or less unsuspectingly, painstaking considerations founded on a proper sence of reality and design precision, are paramount. Thus meaningless hollows, hard edges are care-*

less protruberances (like the fancy and far too low metal posts on Damrak are unnecessarily dangerous) *.

To regard buildings and cities as magic containers which can be filled according to incidental circumstances, is to renounce all sense of specific quality. 'Bigness', that most recent millennial notion, 'allows' whatever is thrown in to be robbed of its identity – neutralizing all and sundry. Nothing will settle into the right place and belong to where it is put; nothing and NOBODY.

As to 'XL', it neither fits nor suits anything or anybody and is therefore 'too small' for everyone and everything (in the eyes of our omnitech-architects, buildings are the largest kind of detail – horrid paradox).

However, if, instead of coming up with hollow grandeur (following their second nature) or, as an alternative, with hollow containers, they would start orchestrating urban components – small and large – providing all the meaningful detailing required – continuously and from place to place – then our cities could no doubt still be saved from autocadding into cyberspace.

Architects, urbanists and those called upon to pay the bill: How about regarding detailing as a habit you cherish most.

---

* *Actually the entire recent urbanistic mismanagement on Damrak demonstrates the present deplorable level of thinking among architects and planners, not merely because of one-way car traffic between Centraal Station and Dam would only 'feel' reasonable if trains were only to leave the station but never to enter it! Besides, the three emphatically separated channels for cars, trams and pedestrians, along shops that are barely presentable, are extremely offensive. As for the lamp-posts etcetera – like those around the Nieuwmarkt – are they not insane?*

READING AMSTERDAM
JOHN THACKARA

Countless modern writers have described the aliena-
tion people feel in modern cities. Psychologists have
discovered a reason for it: having a clear mental picture
of an environment contributes to our mental well-
being, they say, and such clear pictures are often absent
in modern cities. They are hard to 'read', and that
makes us feel uneasy.

There are different ways of locating yourself within
a city and of reading it. In some cities – New York, for
example, and Paris – you can read the streets directly:
because they are organized on a grid, or around huge
boulevards, it is usually easy to orient yourself. In other
cities, for instance London, which grew out of an
agglomeration of villages, no obvious grand plan is
visible at street level, and you need a map.

Amsterdam confronts the visitor with its own brand
of perceptual confusion. As it is old and small, with
only 700,000 inhabitants, you would think it would be
easy to find your way around. Far from it. Something

about the canals is uniquely disorienting. Amsterdam's horse shoe-shaped waterways act like faulty compasses, and lead strangers on long detours because most people probably assume that water moves in a straight line.

Attractions · Many guidebooks make things worse by focusing on lists of 'attractions'. This approach ignores the overall structure of the city; it also obscures the economic and cultural histories which are often the only way of understanding why a city is organized the way it is. Changing patterns of trade, the rise and fall of different economic interests, and the impact of new technologies on mobility and communications – all these factors determine the processes of cities.

The same goes for the buildings that fill them. The better architectural guides explain the contexts in which buildings were conceived and made; but more often, a building is simply labelled with a 'style', or stamped by a plaque bearing the name of its architect. Architectural details can be more informative: for instance, the different patterns of brickwork, the shape of doorknobs, the design of iron railings, the varied use of coloured glass and ceramic tiles, or the way in which a footpath is constructed. Amsterdam cannot boast the rich artisanal traditions of Paris or London, which were manufacturing as well as trading capitals; but the city's urban 'equipment' is nonetheless a source of endless fascination and insight.

However, cities like Amsterdam do not just speak through their hardware. A multi media sea of business and commercial information also plays an important role in the way we experience the city. Posters, signs and bumper stickers. Shop windows and neon displays. Slogans on T-shirts, hats and sports shoes. Discarded packaging and carrier bags. Sales messages on vehicles and billboards. Newspapers in the gutter. Radio commercials blaring out of cars. Logo-covered dirigibles. Junk mail under windscreen wipers. Old men carrying sandwich boards. Newspaper vendors wearing lapel buttons. Leaflets sticking out of letter-boxes. Big Mac cartons. Election stickers in windows.

These multiple layers of printed and inscribed information are seldom described in the guidebooks. They are largely ignored by the planners and they receive insufficient attention from the city fathers – except as a 'trash' problem. Because commercial information is transient – it is not a fixed part of the urban fabric – it tends to be ignored. This is crazy: citizens and visitors alike get more input and stimulation from urban information than from all the landmark buildings and parks combined.

Pollution · Some critics do complain about 'semiotic pollution' – the superabundance of in-your-face signs and messages that the city-dweller cannot ignore. Occasionally, people measure it. A few years ago in New York, before advertising the product, the importer of 'Absolut Vodka' decided to analyse the 'media environment' surrounding the typical yuppie vodka drinker in Manhattan. His researchers set out to measure the quantity and type of commercial messages to which a typical consumer was exposed. On the first morning of the first day, they lost count when the total for most subjects shot over the 400 mark. That's 1,000 or more messages a day.

Similar levels of semiotic pollution occur in parts of Amsterdam. The visitor arriving by train, for example, is confronted at the exit of Centraal Station by Damrak, a gaudy avenue filled with low-price shops for low-budget tourists: fast-food shops, pizza parlours, *Bureaux de Change* and – essential to every family outing – a Museum of Torture. To your left is a canal-side row of picturesque old buildings, replete with ornate mouldings and variegated window designs – just what you'd hope to see having read those tourist brochures. But opposite these buildings, leading away from the station towards Dam Square – the city's traditional centre – is a frenzy of plastic signage and sleazy detritus. So gaudy is this street that it is easy to miss altogether H.P. Berlage's Beurs building on the left-hand side of the street: one of the country's finest historical buildings is shouted down by the informational grunge of the shopping precinct that faces it.

The irony is that if you live in one of the old buildings off to the left, and you seek permission to modify the design of a window or the ornamental brickwork, and your proposal deviates from the way it looked in the seventeenth century, then the feared Monuments Commission, which zealously guards the city's architectural heritage, will almost certainly turn your request down. If, on the other hand, you want to open a shop selling sex-toys, which will be clearly visible to passing children, and if you decide to advertise its presence by large plastic neon signs hanging over the pavement, the evidence of Damrak suggests that you will be allowed to do so. Here are two types of information

Damrak

Lamp-post, Damrak [Schabracq & Postma, 1992]

sitting side by side: near-perfectly preserved old buildings – representing culture, wealth and respectability – face to face with tatty shops, dogshit, sleazy signs and filthy pavements – representing, what? The sanctity of commerce? Liberal politics? It's hard to say.

It's not that the city authorities are oblivious to the importance of designing urban hardware carefully. The installation of strange, geometrical yet asymmetrical bollards and lamp-posts down the middle of Damrak provoked a fearful controversy a couple of years ago. City Hall was wounded: 'But you asked us to attend to the design of this important street', they told the citizenry, 'and now that we have done so, you all complain!'

Schiphol · If you fly to Amsterdam, you have a quite different experience. Arriving at any airport is a brutal test of the way a city deals with information, and Amsterdam's Schiphol does it better than almost any

*Schiphol
Plaza*

other airport in the world. Airports are incredibly com-
plicated places, being saturated with information,
equipment and people. In Schiphol's case, some 40,000
staff come and go every day, quite apart from several
million passengers each year. Making airports easy to
use and understand for passengers from a hundred different countries, who are tired, stressed and befuddled
by hours in the air, is an enormous challenge.

At Schiphol, architectural space and signs are
smoothly integrated. The large yellow signs, and the
banks of video information screens, are strategically
located so that you never feel lost. The transition from
aircraft, through immigration and customs, to the
arrivals hall and cars, taxis and trains is smooth. The
process has an almost calming effect. If you are going to
be processed by a system, better to be processed by an
elegant, even beautiful system than by a bad one.

The typography of the signs at Schiphol, and of the
direction signs beside the motorway into town, is

exemplary. It is most noticeable when you drive into Holland from Belgium: one minute you are driving past a hotchpotch of badly laid-out motorway signs, some illegible, others hanging off their posts; then, as you join the Dutch motorway system, the surfaces suddenly become smooth, and the road signs begin to make sense and deliver coherent, consistent information.

Public patronage · The high standard of 'public design' in the Netherlands is in stark contrast to most European countries, where the best design is commissioned by the private sector – retailers, restaurants and the like. Not so in what the Japanese call 'Super-Modern Holland'. Enlightened public patronage can be seen everywhere: the smartest and most innovative logos and signs nearly all belong to former public bodies such as PTT (post and telephone company) or the railways. If you ever get a chance to see a local resident's gas bill, or tax return, grab it: these official documents are, in design terms, works of art.

Time and again, the information landscape of Amsterdam reminds you that while public services should be well designed, private ones need not. Thus the city's information design is a social and political education. The sleazy mess of the city's central public spaces – Damrak, Leidseplein, Rembrandtplein – is evidence of different standards for public and private activities. Commercial activities pollute carefully regulated public spaces because interference in business would be considered sacrilege in this prosperous trading nation.

PTT *design on Spui* [1996]

Reflections · Being an architect who has always been interested in architectural detailing, I feel comfortable in Amsterdam because in that city one is simply obliged to be interested in details.

The city's landscape exhibits a great variety of materials, a true game with materials (stone, terracotta, steel) in pavements and façades, and one soon discovers that there are details that have become icons. I am referring to those elements which do not owe their impact to their aesthetic qualities, but to the way in which they are related to people's customs and habits.

Highly characteristic is the care with which pedestrians are guided through the city. It is astonishing to see how, in a subtle way, railings follow the movement of pedestrians, go up and down, move around corners and stop in time at places where other systems take over. This is emphasized by the robustness of the detailing. For many years, there has been a tendency to oversize details, whatever the material. It seems to be deliberate, and is not done for physical but for psychological reasons: the strength of the detailing seems to be designed to reassure people. Perhaps this has to do with Amsterdam's historical, maritime environment.

With respect to the latter, one important, though banal, observation needs to be made concerning the intimate relationship between the city and the water. In Amsterdam, both the architecture and the weather are often greyish. Aldo van Eyck's Hubertushuis (1978), in which colour is an element of dialogue between the building and its surroundings, is a rare exception. If in people's recollections of Amsterdam the city is full of colour, then this is generally due to the colour added to the city by that which takes place on the water.

Many of these considerations have influenced our design for the new science centre Impuls. Because it is being built on a pier in an old harbour basin, all architectural detailing has to fit in with the family of details of a busy, typically Amsterdam maritime environment. The building will be surrounded by all kinds of boats, both historical boats and ordinary, functional working vessels. Masts and stays, cranes and industry will influence the experience of the scale of the building. The colour of the building, bright green oxidized copper, has been chosen as a gesture to the colour of the ships floating in the harbour.

As is the case in Genoa, where I was born, the port of Amsterdam is situated in the centre of the city. This means that the image of the city is characterized by water and ships, that is, by reflections, movement, nonpermanency. It is a beautiful pair of notions: a historic city is, even in its details, fundamentally characterized by temporariness and constant change.

DETAILS FROM A STYLE
NORMAN DILWORTH

In London it would take me forty minutes to cross the city to see a friend – by car of course. No one in their right mind would walk or cycle. There is no ease to the city. What greater contrast could you have than Amsterdam, where the car is openly discouraged and you are happily obliged to walk or get out on your bike.

Walking through the city, that is to say along the canals, newly arrived you can easily get lost or find yourself going round in circles. If you don't know, I have to explain that Amsterdam is made up of a series of concentric half circles, like a section of a tree trunk; every hundred years since 1500 it has grown a new canal backed by housing. At first, you find it difficult to get directly from one place to another and one bridge looks the same as another, until you begin to appreciate the subtlety of the city and recognize its landmarks. These landmarks are not ostentatious. They have to do with description or emphasis, marking changes of style or use. They can be both functional and decorative.

The Dutch are masters at utilizing space. Small spaces have to be managed well and what the Dutch can fit into a one-roomed flat defies belief. Their interior design is without equal and this interior close control spreads outward, so that the whole townscape becomes one well-ordered house. We in England have a surfeit of space (or so we have always thought) and that we squander. It has never been necessary to have 'a place for everything and everything in its place'. If you are running a tight-ship, attention to detail becomes para-mount. Sculpture and decoration must be given their place, which in some way means integrated.

Common source · In the years before the First World War, a movement began in Amsterdam which at-tempted to follow a course in which all aspects of design would be totally linked through a common source and would be based on the repetition of details. Integration in the Netherlands has never been that flowing amorphous mass of the Baroque, and here Dutch and English values do have some parallels. Like Gerrit Rietveld's chair, each single element, big or small, is allowed to exist in its own right, while at the same time it is seen as part of a greater whole. The English way is similar, in that part is added to part with each retaining its own character, but it is more pragmatic and the outcome less predictable.

London houses are constructed with joists running from front to back. Party-walls built by labourers were not thought strong enough to take the weight of floors and joists. The good walls (those that could be seen) were built by real brickies. It is not easy to remove the façade from these buildings.

In Amsterdam, joists run from side to side and the façade is easy to replace without disturbing the framework. Eventually, laws were passed to prevent anyone meddling with the exterior without permission. The most extraordinary things go on behind these façades, but over this there is less control. The façade is an indication of what happens within, though not always an expression of it, and the indication can be out of date.

Early this century a committee was called into being to exercise control over the design of new façades, with the aim of maintaining aesthetic harmony with existing buildings. In order to circumvent these regulations some private builders and speculators (i.e., Amstels Bouw Vereeniging) commissioned members of the committee to dress their buildings with acceptable façades.

This committee, the Schoonheidscommissie, was heavily biased towards architects of the Amsterdam School, a number of whom served as members. These architects cannot have been too happy to find themselves working with such superficiality. They had visions of an expression that demanded complete control. Luckily, they soon gained political support and within a few years the group's influence had spread across the city; and how they delighted in their strange and wonderful animal/vegetable details.

This period witnessed a shift from agriculture to industry. As a result, the population of Amsterdam swelled such that it became a matter of urgency to find quick inexpensive solutions to the overwhelming housing problem. Watergraafsmeer, a suburb of Amsterdam, was one of a number of new estates added on to the old city.

◄
*Bridge over
Singelgracht
near
Leidseplein*
[P.L. Kramer,
J. Polet, 1925]

Betondorp

This housing scheme was influenced by Ebenezer Howard's concept of the garden city. Moreover, for the first time, prefabricated concrete slabs were used. These unit structures answered the need for a fast and easy construction technique, but led to simplified forms with little decoration. The suburb, which became universally and prosaically known as 'Betondorp' (concrete village), provides us with an insight into the beginning of a forceful new style that still graces the metropolis.

Detail and decoration · At this distance in time, the similarities between housing schemes built by members of the De Stijl group and the architecture of Betondorp are more evident than their differences, but comparison brings to the fore questions of detail and decoration.

Here were architects of the Amsterdam School, expressionists, having to work with an imposed simplicity. They had only limited control over the form of the building. Method as well as finance dictated a simple approach. For J.J.P. Oud and his colleagues this could only have been seen as a virtue, but for architects such as D. Greiner and J. Gratama it must have been extremely frustrating. And here and there within the estate we catch glimpses of their frustration breaking out in small pockets of ornamentation.

The character of the buildings is formed by their systematic structure, even if the structural units themselves are not always visible. The interlocking nature of these units can be seen in details where it is allowed to be expressive, and here links with the De Stijl group, R. van 't Hoff in particular, are clearly in evidence. However, the Amsterdam School still managed to re-assert itself in the use of these functional features as themes for decoration!

These times were a melting pot of the questions inherent in the integration of art and architecture. Should a line be drawn between the two? The Amsterdam School thought not, others disagreed. Built in the twenties, Betondorp reflects the confusion of opinion. Art is used as decoration and description (carved figures representing various professions), or to punctuate the buildings and provide points of orientation. The two birds at the beginning of Veeteeltstraat, marking an entrance to the estate, are an imaginative contribution, but are not integrated in that inseparable way called for by the Amsterdam School.

Dutch character · To an outsider, Betondorp brings together some of the facets that we see as constituting the Dutch character. And if making the most of a little is something we readily associate with the architects and

Farmer in stone, Betondorp

interior designers of the Netherlands, let us consider one aspect that I myself find peculiar to this city of Amsterdam.

Anywhere else, the corner of a building is just an angle where two planes meet and there is nothing more to be said about it. Here, a corner is an opportunity for fantasy, and how you turn that corner is considered important. Let us look at a design by two leading members of the Amsterdam School, the apartment block on the corner of Burgemeester Tellegenstraat and P.L. Takstraat. It begins at ground level in the usual way, but as it climbs into space it starts to produce fronds which curl inwards and outwards, revealing a tall central stem with at its apex the words 'De Dageraad' (which means 'dawn', but is also the name of the housing corporation that commissioned the block). A seemingly normal corner has thus undergone an extraordinary transformation, gradually dissolving into the upper atmosphere.

This organically shaped building is one of a pair by M. de Klerk and P.L. Kramer and comes close to their ideal of the unity of architecture and sculpture. To complete the concept, similar forms would be repeated inside and outside, extending to all aspects of interior design and furniture in a total work of art. These architects have had a powerful impact on the appearance of Amsterdam, from bridges to letter-boxes – a string of details forming a network of charming, eccentric inventions.

In *The Amsterdam School* (Wim de Wit, ed., Cambridge, Mass., 1983), Maristella Casciato has written that De Klerk 'charged his architecture with multiple symbols, signs and suggestions capable of arresting the decline of (the city's) identity', and in large measure, together with his companions, he succeeded. Amsterdam is not given to grand architectural statements. Its visual vitality has been engendered over the centuries by subtle differences of style and innovation.

De Dageraad [P.L. Kramer, 1922]

Duality · Detail in architecture has a dual function. For the designer, it is a means of averting chaos and of controlling, or even preventing, the surprises which are inherent in construction.

For the viewer of architecture, it is important that even the smallest component of a building, in its dialogue with other details, is part of a consistent whole.

Sources

ARCAM: p. 128

Van Berkel & Bos: p. 98

Nico Bick: pp. 12, 18, 21, 28, 32, 38 (below), 44, 46, 53, 62, 69,
71 (below), 76, 78, 81, 83, 84, 86, 88, 90 (below), 92, 94, 96, 99,
104, 106 (above), 108, 111, 112, 113, 116, 118, 119, 121, 122,
123, 125, 126, 130, 136, 139, 140, 144, 150, 153, 156 (Housing
KNSM-laan, Jo Coenen, 1995), 158, 160, 162 (above), 165,
172 (Van Gogh Museum, Rietveld, Van Dillen, Van Tricht, 1973),
174, 180, 181, 182, 186, 194, 196 (Ajax facilities, René van Zuuk,
1996)

Christine Cadin: p. 191

Adriaan Geuze: p. 30 (Seeds of elm tree, 1996)

Han van Gool, Gemeentelijk buro Monumentenzorg: 64, 74

Cary Markerink: pp. 8, 15, 16 (Front garden, Churchill-laan), 23, 24,
25, 26, 56 (Roof-pavillion Metz & Co, G.Th. Rietveld, 1933), 65,
90 (above), 100, 102, 106 (below), 114, 132, 133, 135, 137, 151,
154, 162 (below), 166, 167, 168, 169, 178, 184, 190, 193

Wim Ruigrok: cover

Dirk Sijmons: pp. 47, 48, 49, 50, 52, 53

Sjoerd Soeters: p. 142

Joop van Stigt: pp. 34, 35, 38 (above), 40

Henk Zantkuijl/Erwin de Maar: pp. 61, 63, 66, 67, 68, 71 (above), 73